United States Government Accountability Office

Report to Congressional Requesters

I0448846

July 2013

AVIATION

Status of DOT's Actions to Address the Future of Aviation Advisory Committee's Recommendations

GAO Highlights

Highlights of GAO-13-657, a report to congressional requesters

AVIATION

Status of DOT's Actions to Address the Future of Aviation Advisory Committee's Recommendations

Why GAO Did This Study

The aviation industry is important to the U.S. economy and is a critical link in the nation's transportation infrastructure. However, the industry has faced challenges, such as an outdated national air-traffic management system and an increasingly competitive global market. In 2010, in response to these and other challenges, DOT established the FAAC to develop a manageable, actionable list of recommendations for DOT. In April 2011, the FAAC released a report outlining 23 recommendations in five areas: environment, financing, competitiveness and viability, labor and workforce, and safety.

GAO was asked to review the status of DOT's efforts to implement the FAAC recommendations. GAO examined 10 of the FAAC's 23 recommendations to determine (1) DOT's progress in addressing the selected recommendations, and any planned future actions; (2) the FAAC members' perspective on the extent to which DOT's actions address these recommendations; and (3) the challenges, if any, that DOT faces in addressing the recommendations. The 10 selected recommendations covered each of the 5 areas and allowed GAO to leverage ongoing or recent GAO work. GAO did not analyze the validity of the FAAC's recommendations, and our work does not take a position on, or represent an endorsement of, the recommendations. GAO reviewed agency documents and literature, and interviewed FAAC members and DOT and FAA officials. DOT provided technical comments, which were incorporated as appropriate.

View GAO-13-657. For more information, contact Gerald L. Dillingham, Ph.D., at (202) 512-2834 or dillinghamg@gao.gov.

What GAO Found

While the Department of Transportation (DOT) is not required to implement the Future of Aviation Advisory Committee (FAAC) recommendations, DOT and the Federal Aviation Administration (FAA) have taken actions on the 10 FAAC recommendations that GAO reviewed (see table). DOT and FAA officials noted that they continue to work on three recommendations as part of long-term efforts and have ongoing work related to some of the seven recommendations that they believe are addressed.

FAAC members recognized DOT's actions to address the recommendations. However, a majority of the FAAC subcommittee members believe that more work remains to fully address 9 of the 10 recommendations (see table). FAAC members stated that some recommendations may not be fully addressed because they are linked to ongoing efforts that DOT also identified.

DOT, FAA officials, and FAAC members most frequently identified resource constraints and the need to collaborate with multiple stakeholders as implementation challenges and in some cases, noted efforts to address these challenges. DOT officials noted that fully addressing some recommendations may depend on factors outside of DOT's control, such as extending the alternative minimum tax exemption, which would require legislation, and developing sustainable alternative fuels, which is a long-term, multi-agency effort.

Status of FAAC Recommendations Selected for GAO Review

Area and selected FAAC recommendations	Status per DOT/FAA officials	Status per majority of FAAC members
Environment		
Exercise strong national leadership to promote U.S. aviation as a first user of sustainable alternative fuels	In progress	In progress
Establish a harmonized approach for aviation carbon dioxide emission reductions	In progress	In progress
Financing		
Support extending the alternative minimum tax (AMT) exemption for airport private activity bonds	Addressed	In progress
Fund accelerated Next Generation Air Transportation System equipage of aircraft	Addressed	In progress
Review eligibility criteria for the Airport Improvement Program and Passenger Facility Charge Program	Addressed	In progress
Competitiveness and viability		
Promote the global competitiveness of the U.S. aviation industry	In progress	In progress
Labor and workforce		
Ensure coordination and focus on science, technology, engineering, and math (STEM) education programs	Addressed	Addressed
Safety		
Seek legal protections for safety data	Addressed	In progress
Support predictive analytic capabilities for safety data	Addressed	In progress
Review and reprioritize FAA's rulemaking initiatives	Addressed	In progress

Source: GAO analysis of DOT/FAA and FAAC member interviews.

_____ **United States Government Accountability Office**

Contents

Tables

Abbreviations

ADS-B	Automatic Dependent Surveillance-Broadcast
ACE	Aviation Career Education
AIP	Airport Improvement Program
AMT	alternative minimum tax
ARAC	Aviation Rulemaking Advisory Committee
ASAP	Aviation Safety Action Program
ASIAS	Aviation Safety Information Analysis and Sharing
ATOS	Air Transportation Oversight System
AVSED	Aviation and Space Education
CAAFI	Commercial Aviation Alternative Fuels Initiative
CLEEN	Continuous Lower Energy, Emissions, and Noise
CoSTEM	Committee on Science, Technology, Engineering, and Math Education
CO_2	carbon dioxide
DataComm	Data Communications
DOD	Department of Defense
DOE	Department of Energy
DOT	Department of Transportation
EPA	Environmental Protection Agency

ETS	Emissions Trading Scheme
EU	European Union
FAA	Federal Aviation Administration
FAAC	Future of Aviation Advisory Committee
FACA	Federal Advisory Committee Act
FOQA	Flight Operational Quality Assurance
HEFA	Hydroprocessed Esters and Fatty Acids
ICAO	International Civil Aviation Organization
NAC	NextGen Advisory Committee
NC3	National Coalition of Certification Centers
NextGen	Next Generation Air Transportation System
NSTC	National Science and Technology Council
NTSB	National Transportation Safety Board
OSTP	Office of Science and Technology Policy
PBN	Performance-Based Navigation
PFC	Passenger Facility Charge
PREP	Pre-Rulemaking Evaluation and Prioritization
RAISE	Recognizing Aviation and Aerospace Innovation in Science and Engineering
RFS2	Renewable Fuel Standard
RITA	Research and Innovative Technology Administration
RPWG	Rulemaking Prioritization Working Group
STEM	science, technology, engineering, and math
SMS	safety management system
USDA	United States Department of Agriculture
WAM	Wide Area Multilateration

July 25, 2013

Congressional Requesters

Over the past decade, the aviation industry has faced fluctuating oil prices, an economic recession, and safety concerns following the crash of a Colgan Air flight in Buffalo, New York, as well as ongoing changes in the industry related to air-traffic control modernization, increased global competition, and an aging workforce. On November 12, 2009, the Secretary of the Department of Transportation (DOT) convened an Aviation Summit to gather industry and expert opinion on actions that would promote future success of the aviation industry. The discussion centered on five areas: environment, financing, competitiveness and viability, labor and workforce, and safety. With these areas in mind, Secretary Ray LaHood chartered the Future of Aviation Advisory Committee (FAAC) on April 16, 2010, to develop a manageable, actionable list of recommendations in each of these five areas for DOT. The FAAC included 19 members—1 government official and 18 non-government representatives—from a cross-section of stakeholders, such as air carriers, airports, airline labor unions, manufacturers, and representatives from the finance community, academia, and passenger interests. On April 11, 2011, the FAAC issued a final report listing 23 recommendations that the FAAC identified as critical to the future of the U.S. aviation industry.

You asked us to review the status of DOT's efforts to implement the FAAC recommendations. We examined 10 of the FAAC's 23 recommendations to determine (1) DOT's progress in addressing the selected recommendations and any further planned actions; (2) the FAAC members' perspectives on the extent to which DOT's actions address these recommendations; and (3) the challenges, if any, that DOT faces in addressing the recommendations. The 10 selected recommendations cover each of the 5 areas reviewed by the FAAC and allowed us to leverage ongoing or recently completed GAO work. Given that the 10 recommendations are directed toward specific, discrete actions, our statements regarding DOT's progress in addressing the recommendations are specific to each recommendation and cannot be generalized to assess DOT's overall progress across all 23 FAAC recommendations.[1] We did not analyze the validity of the commission's recommendations, and our work does not take a position on, or represent an endorsement of, the recommendations. See table 1 for a list of the recommendations we reviewed.

Table 1: FAAC Recommendations Selected for GAO Review

Area	FAAC recommendations
Environment	• Exercise strong national leadership to promote and showcase U.S. aviation as a first user of sustainable alternative fuels
	• Establish a harmonized approach for aviation carbon dioxide emission reductions
Financing	• Support extending the alternative minimum tax exemption for airport private activity bonds
	• Fund accelerated Next Generation Air Transportation System (NextGen)[a] equipage of aircraft
	• Review eligibility criteria for the Airport Improvement Program and Passenger Facility Charge Program
Competitiveness and viability	• Promote the global competitiveness of the U.S. aviation industry
Labor and workforce	• Ensure coordination and focus on science, technology, engineering, and math (STEM) education programs
Safety	• Seek legal protections for safety data program participants
	• Support predictive analytic capabilities for safety data and information[b]
	• Review and reprioritize FAA's rulemaking initiatives

Source: FAAC report.

[a]The Federal Aviation Administration (FAA), in collaboration with other federal agencies and the aviation industry, is transforming the nation's ground-based air-traffic control system to an air-traffic management system using satellite-based navigation and other technology. This transformation is referred to as the Next Generation Air Transportation System (NextGen).

[b]This recommendation is related to FAA's efforts to shift toward a proactive, data-driven safety oversight approach, commonly referred to as a safety management system (SMS) approach.

To determine DOT's progress and challenges in addressing the selected recommendations, we reviewed relevant GAO and DOT Office of Inspector General reports, agency documents, including plans for addressing the recommendations, DOT and Federal Aviation Administration (FAA) documentation of actions taken, and DOT's website for tracking progress on the committee's recommendations. We also reviewed legislation to determine the extent to which it affected or addressed the recommendations. In addition, we interviewed DOT and FAA officials about the steps they have taken to address the recommendations and any challenges they have faced in implementing the recommendations. We also interviewed 17 of the 18 FAAC non-

[1]See appendix I for a complete list of all 23 recommendations from the FAAC.

government members to obtain their perspectives on the extent to which DOT's actions addressed the recommendations from the subcommittees on which they served, any challenges DOT faces in addressing the recommendations, and what, if any, additional actions DOT should take to address the recommendations.[2] Although DOT is not required to implement any of the FAAC's recommendations, we solicited the committee members' perspective on whether DOT should continue monitoring and reporting on its progress in addressing the recommendations. A list of the FAAC members we interviewed is available in appendix II.

We conducted this performance audit from November 2012 through July 2013 in accordance with generally accepted government auditing standards. Those standards require that we plan and perform the audit to obtain sufficient, appropriate evidence to provide a reasonable basis for our findings and conclusions based on our audit objectives. We believe that the evidence obtained provides a reasonable basis for our findings and conclusions based on our audit objectives.

Background

The U.S. aerospace industry contributes to the nation's economic health and national security. The industry's wide-ranging activities—including aircraft manufacturing and commercial aviation—make it a major contributor to U.S. economic growth. DOT and the FAA (an administration of DOT) each play a policy and regulatory role in aviation, with DOT involved in consumer and economic issues, such as licensing airlines and reviewing applications for antitrust immunity between airlines, and FAA's overseeing the safety of civil aviation. To inform these efforts, various administrations and Congresses have periodically established committees or commissions comprised of external stakeholders to provide recommendations for DOT and FAA, as well as other agencies involved in aviation, to consider in their implementation of aviation policy. For example, in 1996, President Clinton established the White House Commission on Aviation Safety and Security, which provided 57 recommendations in the areas of safety, air traffic control, security, and accident response. In 2001, Congress established the Commission on the Future of the United States Aerospace Industry to study issues associated with the future of this industry in the global economy, and to

---

[2]One FAAC member was not available for an interview.

recommend potential actions by the federal government to support the maintenance of a robust aerospace industry in the 21st century.[3]

In contrast to these two efforts, the FAAC was established as a federal advisory committee, subject to the Federal Advisory Committee Act (FACA).[4] Federal advisory committees exist throughout the executive branch of the federal government, providing input and advice to agencies in a variety of ways, such as preparing reports and developing recommendations. GAO has noted that advisory committees can be effective tools for agencies to gather input on topics of interest by informing agency leaders about issues of importance to the agencies' missions, consolidating input from multiple sources, and providing input at a relatively low cost.[5] While an advisory group's input or recommendations may form the basis for a federal agency's decisions or policies, other factors may play a role in determining what action an agency ultimately takes. Because such groups are by design advisory, agencies are not required to implement their advice or recommendations.

On April 16, 2010, Secretary Ray LaHood chartered the FAAC for a one-year term and asked the DOT Assistant Secretary for Aviation and International Affairs to lead the effort. The FAAC was directed to provide information, advice, and recommendations to the Secretary on ensuring the competitiveness of the U.S. aviation industry and its capability to address the evolving transportation needs, challenges, and opportunities of the global economy. The FAAC was comprised of a cross-section of aviation stakeholders. During its first meeting, the Secretary asked the FAAC to develop consensus-based recommendations that could be acted upon immediately or in the near future, with tangible results.[6] He also

---

[3]In 2006, GAO reviewed the progress that federal agencies, including the FAA, had made in addressing the recommendations made by the Commission on the Future of the United States Aerospace Industry. GAO, *U.S. Aerospace Industry: Progress in Implementing Aerospace Commission Recommendations, and Remaining Challenges*, GAO-06-920 (Washington, D.C.: Sept. 13, 2006).

[4]Pub. L. No. 92-463, 86 Stat. 770 (1972), codified, as amended, at 5 U.S.C. app. § 2. The FACA sets forth requirements for FACA advisory groups' formation, their operations, and how they provide advice and recommendations to the federal government.

[5]GAO, *Federal Advisory Groups: DOT and DOE Can Take Steps to Better Assess Duplication Risk and Enhance Usefulness*, GAO-12-472 (Washington, D.C.: Mar. 29, 2012).

[6]Future of Aviation Advisory Committee, *Record of Meeting* (Washington, D.C.: May 25, 2010).

stated that the FAAC should remain cognizant of the tools that DOT and FAA could use to implement the recommendations, such as the federal rulemaking process, proposing legislation to Congress, and recommending compliance measures for industry. The FAAC established subcommittees to develop recommendations in the five areas specified in the FAAC charter: environment, financing, competitiveness and viability, labor and workforce, and safety. The subcommittees met multiple times over the course of 2010, and the full FAAC briefed the Secretary on its 23 recommendations on December 15, 2010, with a final report outlining the recommendations and their underlying rationale released on April 11, 2011.

The Secretary publicly emphasized that the FAAC recommendations would not "sit on a shelf," and DOT established a process to implement the recommendations. DOT officials stated that the Office of Aviation and International Affairs has led DOT's work on addressing the FAAC recommendations and has provided periodic updates to FAAC members. Each recommendation was assigned to an "owner"—DOT or FAA staff—some of whom were already conducting work relevant to the recommendation. DOT officials also noted that some of the recommendations with multiple subactions have more than one owner. DOT staff collaborated with recommendation owners to create a "smart sheet" for addressing each FAAC recommendation. This document provided information on interim goals, or actions that must occur to reach the final goal; beneficiaries and allies of the recommendation; and potential challenges. The owners were not required to update these documents as time progressed. DOT officials stated that for about a year after the FAAC report was released, DOT's Office of Aviation and International Affairs had regular status meetings with the recommendation owners to ascertain their progress, and recommendation owners then reported progress periodically to DOT officials. DOT periodically updates a website on the status of the FAAC recommendations. During the course of our review, we noted that some of the recommendations had not been updated for over one year; however, DOT updated the status of all of the recommendations on its website in June 2013.

DOT and FAA Officials Believe That Seven of the Selected Recommendations Are Addressed and That Three Are In Progress

DOT and FAA have taken actions on the 10 FAAC recommendations we reviewed. DOT and FAA officials noted that 3 of the 10 recommendations we reviewed—sustainable alternative fuels, global competitiveness, and a harmonized approach to carbon dioxide emission reductions—continue to be addressed as part of long-term efforts. For example, DOT officials noted that addressing the global competitiveness recommendation is tied to long-term policy efforts with no timetable for conclusion, such as negotiating agreements with other countries to reduce the barriers for U.S. carriers interested in serving markets in those countries. While officials stated that DOT and FAA have addressed the other seven recommendations, they highlighted ongoing work on issues related to some of these recommendations. For example, FAA officials noted they have addressed the recommendation to accelerate investment and installation of NextGen equipment on aircraft because they are working to develop a program to provide financial incentives and operational benefits to operators that install NextGen equipment early.[7] However, the officials added that they are still working to determine what the program will entail, including soliciting input from aircraft operators and potential private partners to determine how to establish an incentive program that operators want to participate in. They also noted that the appropriations requirements for a credit program have not yet been met. For additional details on actions DOT and FAA have taken on the recommendations, see section 1 of this report.

FAAC Members Acknowledge DOT's Actions but Believe That More Work Remains in Responding to the Selected Recommendations

FAAC members acknowledged DOT and FAA efforts to address the 10 recommendations selected for our work; however, a majority of the FAAC subcommittee members believe more work remains to fully address 9 of the 10 recommendations. See table 2 for a summary of the recommendations as well as their status according to DOT and the FAAC subcommittee members we interviewed.

---

[7]FAA's current NextGen implementation plans include midterm implementation activities through 2020 and the long term to 2025 and beyond.

Table 2: Status of FAAC Recommendations Selected for GAO Review

Area and selected FAAC recommendations	Status per DOT/FAA officials	Status per majority of FAAC members
Environment		
Exercise strong national leadership to promote U.S. aviation as a first user of sustainable alternative fuels	In progress	In progress
Establish a harmonized approach for aviation carbon dioxide emission reductions	In progress	In progress
Financing		
Support extending the alternative minimum tax (AMT) exemption for airport private activity bonds	Addressed	In progress
Fund accelerated Next Generation Air Transportation System equipage of aircraft	Addressed	In progress
Review eligibility criteria for the Airport Improvement Program and Passenger Facility Charge Program	Addressed	In progress
Competitiveness and viability		
Promote the global competitiveness of the U.S. aviation industry	In progress	In progress
Labor and workforce		
Ensure coordination and focus on science, technology, engineering, and math (STEM) education programs	Addressed	Addressed
Safety		
Seek legal protections for safety data	Addressed	In progress
Support predictive analytic capabilities for safety data	Addressed	In progress
Review and reprioritize FAA's rulemaking initiatives	Addressed	In progress

Source: GAO analysis of DOT/FAA and FAAC member interviews.

Similar to DOT and FAA officials, FAAC members stated that some recommendations may not be fully addressed due to the recommendation's being linked to ongoing or long-term efforts. For example, FAAC members noted that DOT and FAA efforts to address the sustainable alternative fuels recommendation require collaborating across many agencies, such as the Department of Energy (DOE), the United States Department of Agriculture (USDA), and the Environmental Protection Agency (EPA), and a continued, long-term federal focus. In some cases, FAAC members stated that DOT and FAA should continue their current efforts to address the recommendations; but some FAAC members felt that DOT and FAA should take additional actions to address certain recommendations. For example, five of the six finance FAAC subcommittee members stated that the recommendation to fund accelerated NextGen equipage of aircraft was not addressed, and two suggested that the department take additional steps to collaborate with industry to design an incentive program and develop a stronger business case for airlines to invest in equipping early. Conversely, five of the seven subcommittee members believe that the department's actions addressed the recommendation on science, technology, engineering, and mathematics (STEM) education. For additional details on FAAC members' perspectives on the DOT and FAA actions to address the recommendations, see section 1 of this report.

While DOT is not required to monitor or report on the status of the FAAC recommendations, 13 of the 17 FAAC members generally agreed that the department should continue monitoring and reporting on the recommendations' status, with some adding that this ensures continued focus on their implementation. On the other hand, two FAAC members stated that DOT should continue reporting only on certain recommendations, such as recommendations that would be implemented over the long term or recommendations it has not addressed. Another FAAC member stated that DOT and FAA should ensure that efforts to address the recommendations become ingrained into the daily work of agency staff, rather than DOT's and FAA's viewing them as a separate effort. The remaining FAAC member stated that DOT should reassess whether it makes sense to continue or close out the effort, adding that as time passes, the recommendations may become irrelevant or unlikely to be addressed. DOT officials told us that for ongoing recommendations, they will continue work on these recommendations and are determining the extent to which it will continue reporting on the status of the recommendations. However, DOT has not yet established a time frame for when it might make such a decision.

Resource Constraints and Stakeholder Collaboration Were Most Frequently Cited as Implementation Challenges for the Selected Recommendations

Resource constraints and the need to collaborate with multiple stakeholders were cited most frequently by DOT and FAA officials, as well as by FAAC members, as implementation challenges. Specifically, DOT and FAA officials or FAAC members identified resource constraints, such as limited funding for programs or staff, as a challenge in implementing 6 of the 10 FAAC recommendations that we reviewed. These 6 include the recommendations pertaining to sustainable fuels, carbon dioxide emission reductions, reviewing eligibility criteria for the Airport Improvement and Passenger Facility Charge Programs, STEM education, predictive safety risk-discovery capability, and prioritizing rulemaking. Agency officials and committee members also explained how constrained resources might affect progress in addressing these recommendations. For example, when discussing the recommendation that DOT and FAA establish a harmonized approach for aviation carbon dioxide emission reductions, FAA officials told us that resource constraints could hamper their ability to conduct necessary research and participate in international forums designed to foster discussion on harmonized regulatory approaches. However, DOT and FAA officials also outlined their methods for operating within these constraints. For example, while noting that funding and limited resources pose challenges to maintaining long-term STEM efforts, officials stated that the agencies work to leverage resources through stakeholder partnerships. In addition, DOT and FAA officials or FAAC members identified challenges in collaborating with and gaining the consensus of a number of stakeholders for four recommendations, those related to sustainable fuels, carbon dioxide emission reductions, global competitiveness, and STEM education. These recommendations range in the type of involvement needed both within and outside DOT and FAA. For example, six of the seven FAAC labor and workforce subcommittee members we interviewed recognized DOT's ongoing efforts on STEM issues require that DOT maintain the participation of outside groups, such as other agencies, industry, and other stakeholders.

However, each recommendation also had unique challenges. For example, with respect to the recommendation that the agencies ensure that safety data submitted by air carriers and other stakeholders is protected from public disclosure, FAAC members noted that despite legal protections provided by recent legislation,[8] industry concerns remain regarding the disclosure of safety data during legal proceedings. FAA officials have recognized that such concerns could limit the implementation of FAA efforts to promote safety management systems, which depend upon the open sharing of safety information among aviation stakeholders.[9] In addition, DOT and FAA officials noted that in some cases they took actions to address the recommendation, but factors beyond DOT's control, such as the need for legislative action, affected DOT's ability to fully implement the recommendation. For example, while the agency supported a provision that would have extended the alternative minimum tax exemption for all private activity bonds, including

[8]FAA Modernization and Reform Act of 2012, Pub. L. No. 112-95, § 310, 126 Stat. 11, 64 (2012).

[9]GAO has reported that FAA is in the midst of a shift toward a proactive, data-driven safety oversight approach, commonly referred to as a safety management system (SMS) approach. Under this new approach, FAA plans to use aviation safety data to identify system-wide trends in aviation safety and manage emerging hazards before they result in incidents or accidents. See GAO, *Aviation Safety: FAA Efforts Have Improved Safety but Challenges Remain in Key Areas*, GAO-13-442T (Washington, D.C.: Apr. 16, 2013).

airport private-activity bonds—as recommended by the FAAC—this provision did not become law. Agency officials view this recommendation as addressed since any further action would require legislative action, and there is not currently a legislative vehicle for this provision.

Section 1 of this report includes the 10 recommendations in our review, detailed discussions of DOT and FAA completed or planned actions to address each of the 10 FAAC recommendations, FAAC members' assessment of DOT and FAA progress, and challenges to implementing each recommendation.

Agency Comments

We provided DOT with a draft of this report for their review and comment. DOT responded by email and provided technical clarifications, which we incorporated into the report as appropriate.

We are sending copies of this report to appropriate congressional committees, the Secretary of Transportation, and interested parties. This report will also be available at no charge on the GAO website at http://www.gao.gov.

Should you or your staff have questions concerning this report, please contact me at (202) 512-2834 or dillinghamg@gao.gov. Contact points for our Offices of Congressional Relations and Public Affairs may be found on the last page of this report. Key contributors to this report are listed in appendix III.

Gerald L. Dillingham, Ph.D.
Director, Physical Infrastructure Issues

List of Requesters

The Honorable John D. Rockefeller IV
Chairman
Committee on Commerce, Science, and Transportation
United States Senate

The Honorable Bill Shuster
Chairman
Committee on Transportation and Infrastructure
House of Representatives

The Honorable Frank A. LoBiondo
Chairman
Subcommittee on Aviation
Committee on Transportation and Infrastructure
House of Representatives

The Honorable John L. Mica
House of Representatives

The Honorable Thomas E. Petri
House of Representatives

Section 1: Selected FAAC Recommendations and DOT's and FAA's Actions to Address Them

This section presents the 10 FAAC recommendations we reviewed and includes detail on DOT and FAA actions to address the recommendations, FAAC members' assessment of DOT and FAA progress on the recommendations, and challenges in implementing each recommendation. Also, we numbered these recommendations for reporting purposes, but these numbers do not align with the numbers assigned to these recommendations in the FAAC report.

Table 3: FAAC Recommendations Selected for GAO Review and Location in Report

Area	FAAC recommendations	Page number
Environment	• Exercise strong national leadership to promote and showcase U.S. aviation as a first user of sustainable alternative fuels	13
	• Establish a harmonized approach for aviation carbon dioxide emission reductions	20
Financing	• Support extending the alternative minimum tax exemption for airport private activity bonds	25
	• Fund accelerated NextGen equipage of aircraft	29
	• Review eligibility criteria for the Airport Improvement Program and Passenger Facility Charge Program	36
Competitiveness and viability	• Promote the global competitiveness of the U.S. aviation industry	42
Labor and workforce	• Ensure coordination and focus on STEM education programs	49
Safety	• Seek legal protections for safety data program participants	57
	• Support predictive analytic capabilities for safety data and information	62
	• Review and reprioritize FAA's rulemaking initiatives	67

Source: FAAC report.

1. FAAC Recommendation— Sustainable Alternative Fuels

Issue Overview

According to the DOT's Transportation and Climate Change Clearinghouse, commercial aircraft accounted for about 2.5 percent of the total U.S. contribution of greenhouse gas emissions in 2006. We reported in June 2009 that global aviation's relative contribution to greenhouse gas emissions is forecasted to grow.[1] The use of alternative fuels, including those derived from biological sources (biofuels), has the potential to reduce greenhouse gas emissions from aircraft in the future. A domestic source of alternative fuels also has the potential to provide energy security to the United States and fuel price stability for airlines. While the federal government has promoted biofuels as an alternative to petroleum-based fuels since the 1970s, advanced biofuels—defined as renewable fuels that meet certain criteria, including ones that use cellulosic feedstocks such as corn stover or switchgrass—are at the earliest stages of being commercially produced in the United States.[2] Numerous logistical and economic challenges, such as developing a sustainable feedstock supply and producing cost-competitive fuels, must be overcome before they are commercially viable. Several federal agencies—including DOT, United States Department of Agriculture (USDA), Department of Energy (DOE), Environmental Protection Agency (EPA), and Department of Defense (DOD)—play a role in developing the supply chain for alternative aviation fuels. Federal agency programs and efforts include support for: research and development; developing new fuel feedstocks, fuel conversion methods, environmental standards, and production methods; scaling up commercial production; and certifying new fuel production pathways. Within DOT, FAA's primary roles include sponsoring research studies; conducting and developing tools for

---

[1]GAO, *Aviation and Climate Change: Aircraft Emissions Expected to Grow, but Technological and Operational Improvements and Government Policies Can Help Control Emissions*, GAO-09-554 (Washington, D.C.: June 8, 2009)

[2]*Feedstock* refers to the raw material from which fuel is derived. Cellulosic feedstocks are a specific type of feedstock that are made of cellulosic (plant-based) materials such as corn stover (the cobs, sta ks, leaves, and husks of corn plants) or switchgrass.

environmental and cost analysis; funding certification and qualification testing to inform efforts by the standard-setting organization ASTM International;[3] and enabling government and aviation industry coordination. FAA officials told us FAA does not have authority or funding to provide financial incentives for development and deployment of alternative aviation fuels. However, other federal agencies—such as the Internal Revenue Service, USDA, and DOE—have administered programs that provide numerous incentives, including subsidies through tax credits, to produce feedstocks, and refine and use biofuels. In its report, the FAAC stated that the aviation industry has unique fuel requirements and is well-positioned to be a national and international leader in the use of sustainable renewable alternative fuels.

The FAAC recommended that DOT exercise strong national leadership to promote and display U.S. aviation as a first user of sustainable alternative fuels and provide increased support for FAA's work on alternative fuels. The FAAC discussed four specific areas in supporting its recommendation.

DOT's and FAA's Actions to Address Recommendation

Table 4 provides a summary of the FAAC recommendation and underlying rationale, and DOT's and FAA's actions to address it, as of June 2013.

---

[3]ASTM International, formerly known as the American Society for Testing and Materials, works to deliver the test methods, specifications, guides, and practices that support industries and governments worldwide.

Table 4: FAAC Recommendation on Sustainable Alternative Fuels and DOT's and FAA's Actions to Address It, as of June 2013

FAAC recommendation—alternative fuels[a]	DOT/FAA actions
Accelerate research and fuel approval—Additional federal support is needed to accelerate the development and approval of jet fuel specifications.[b]	FAA conducts testing that supports the certification and qualification for new alternative aviation jet fuels. These activities are conducted through its Continuous Lower Energy, Emissions, and Noise (CLEEN) program,[c] as well as private contracts. Through these efforts, FAA supported ASTM International's approval of a bio-derived sustainable alternative "drop-in" jet fuel[d] known as Hydroprocessed Esters and Fatty Acids (HEFA) for commercial use in July 2011.[e] As of May 2013, FAA had 8 ongoing testing efforts that are intended to provide data to support certification and qualification of additional "drop-in" jet fuels from renewable sources, including sugars and cellulose.[f] In addition, FAA plans to select a new Center of Excellence that will include a focus on alternative jet fuels later this fall and have it operational by the end of calendar year 2013.[g] FAA is also collaborating with other entities that conduct research supporting alternative aviation fuels, including other federal agencies and international governments, through the Commercial Aviation Alternative Fuels Initiative (CAAFI) as well as direct interaction.[h]
Provide incentives to accelerate development and deployment—It would be of significant help if in addition to FAA's current research funding, it were empowered to provide and promote funding to support deployment of alternative aviation fuels.	Absent new legislation that provides FAA authority and a new funding source, FAA officials noted that they leverage existing mechanisms and funding within other federal agencies by encouraging them to include aviation fuels as part of their own incentive programs. For example, it supports EPA's Renewable Fuel Standard program (RFS2)—which created a credit market for renewable transportation fuels, of which some aviation jet fuels are approved to receive credit—by conducting emissions testing of alternative fuels through one of its Centers of Excellence and providing data that support EPA's approval of new fuels under the program.[i] In addition, through the Farm to Fly initiative and its extension,[j] FAA and USDA have partnered with industry in assisting American farmers in the selection and cultivation of energy crops for conversion into affordable and sustainable aviation biofuels. FAA officials also noted that FAA is coordinating with DOE and DOD on their deployment activities both directly and via CAAFI.
Ensure crediting of environmental benefit at the point of purchase—FAA should work to establish a regulatory structure that will provide the environmental credit to the air carrier purchasing the fuel—commonly referred to as a "book and claim" crediting approach.	FAA officials said that a precursor to developing a regulatory framework for how to credit alternative fuel purchases is to have a recognized method for calculating the credit. As discussed below, FAA undertakes such efforts through its own analyses, as well as collaborating with other agencies on efforts to analyze environmental and economic impacts, as well as sustainability of alternative jet fuels.

FAAC recommendation—alternative fuels[a]	DOT/FAA actions
Ensure accepted environmental criteria for alternative fuels, domestically and internationally—The DOT/FAA should develop and execute a plan, working with government, industry, and other relevant domestic stakeholders to develop and confirm environmental criteria, including associated life-cycle analysis protocols, for aviation alternative fuels. The DOT/FAA should also work to facilitate international acceptance of these criteria so the benefits of alternative aviation fuels can be available domestically and internationally.	As of May 2013, FAA had six on-going efforts—some of which are through one of its Centers of Excellence and the John A. Volpe National Transportation Systems Center—that focus on environmental impacts, economic impacts, feasibility, and sustainability of alternative jet fuels, among other things. FAA also collaborates with other Federal agencies—including DOD, EPA, and DOE—on domestic efforts to develop life-cycle analysis protocols. CAAFI stakeholders are currently examining how CO_2 emissions would differ under different policies and regulatory assumptions, including those under EPA's RFS2 program and the European Union's renewable energy directive. FAA follows international efforts and shares best practices with the United Nation's International Civil Aviation Organization (ICAO) and other countries. For example, FAA has formal agreements to cooperate with Australia, Brazil, Germany, and Spain on issues related to alternative aviation fuels.

Source: FAAC report and GAO analysis of FAA documents and interviews.

[a]The FAAC recommended that DOT exercise strong national leadership to promote and display U.S. aviation as a first user of sustainable alternative fuels and provide increased support for FAA's work on alternative fuels. The FAAC discussed four specific areas in supporting its recommendation.

[b]FAA does not certify aviation fuel, rather FAA certifies that aircraft, including engines and accessories, meet FAA airworthiness standards. Those standards require engines to use fuels that meet specific ASTM standards.

[c]FAA's CLEEN program is an effort to accelerate development and commercial deployment of environmentally promising aircraft technologies and sustainable alternative fuels. CLEEN is part of NextGen, FAA's program to transform the nation's ground-based air-traffic control system to an air-traffic management system using satellite-based navigation and other advanced technology.

[d]"Drop-in" means that the fuel can be used without changes to aircraft systems or fueling infrastructure.

[e]This approval was for a 50 percent blend of HEFA jet fuel with Jet A.

[f]FAA provides data to five working groups within ASTM International that are currently each looking at a new potential alternative jet fuel pathway.

[g]FAA issued a final solicitation for the new Center of Excellence, which closed March 20, 2013. Establishment of the Center was permitted under the FAA Modernization and Reform Act, Pub. L. No. 112-95, § 911(d), 126 Stat. 11, 142.

[h]CAAFI is a coalition of airlines, aircraft and engine manufacturers, energy producers, researchers, international participants, and U.S. government agencies seeking to enhance energy security and environmental sustainability for aviation by exploring the use of alternative jet fuels.

[i]In 2010, EPA approved jet fuel pathways under the RFS2 program, and in March 2013, EPA clarified that these jet fuel pathways qualify for credits as renewable diesel.

[j]The Farm to Fly initiative brought together the U.S. aviation community, government stakeholders, USDA, DOE, DOT, and DOD, to express unified support for the President's goals of environmental stewardship and energy independence, and furthered a commitment of resources dedicated to research and development and deployment through public-sector leadership and financial incentives to bring production online. The Secretaries of Agriculture and Transportation joined others on April 15, 2013, to sign a 5-year extension agreement of the Farm to Fly initiative.

DOT's and FAA's Planned Actions

FAA officials told us they view actions to address this recommendation as a long-term effort given that its goals for the development of alternative aviation fuels—that is, for the U.S. aviation industry to displace 1-billion gallons of petroleum jet fuel with alternative jet fuel by 2018 and to achieve carbon neutral growth by 2020 (baseline year of 2005)—are several years or more away. Because of the long-term nature of this effort, officials told us they plan to continue FAA's research and collaboration with other agencies, industry groups, and other countries.

FAAC Members' Assessment of DOT's and FAA's Progress

All five of the FAAC environmental subcommittee members we interviewed expressed support for FAA's actions to address this recommendation, adding that fully addressing this recommendation will require a long-term, ongoing effort and collaboration with a number of parties. For example, some subcommittee members identified additional actions that they think FAA or the federal government should take in response to this recommendation. Two subcommittee members noted the need for an increased federal focus on supporting the deployment and commercial viability of alternative fuels through tax incentives, public-private partnerships, direct support, or other means to encourage industry to invest its capital. One subcommittee member stated that while DOT or FAA may not have the statutory authority to provide incentives to accelerate development and deployment, they should explore their authority to support additional deployment activities. In our discussions with FAA officials on this issue, they stated that FAA has not sought direct authority for these activities because they believe that it is a wiser use of federal resources to use existing federal support mechanisms that are funded by USDA and DOE. Another subcommittee member stated that more overall federal funding is needed for research on conversion technology and getting through the fuel approval process, and that the research projects that receive federal funding should be focused specifically on producing the data needed for fuel approval, rather than addressing broader issues. In addition, this subcommittee member stated that FAA should increase its outreach and collaboration with other groups such as the Sustainable Aviation Fuel Users Group, the Sustainable Aviation Biofuels for Brazil effort, and the Midwest Aviation Sustainable Biofuels Initiative. According to FAA officials, the agency is engaged in the latter two initiatives.

Challenges in Implementing the Recommendation

- **Resource constraints**. FAA officials and two of the subcommittee members stated that resources, specifically funding for the programs and staff time to work on the projects, pose a challenge in addressing this recommendation. Subcommittee members raised concerns about budget uncertainty affecting the agencies' abilities to support long-term efforts in this area.

- **Scalable, affordable, and sustainable fuel supply**. FAA officials and two subcommittee members also pointed out the challenges related to scalability—that is, being able to produce sufficient quantities of alternative aviation fuel at a reasonable price. FAA officials noted that building a sustainable supply chain would be a challenge. However, officials said that the production activities by USDA, DOE, and DOD could help establish the market, and the programs at DOE, EPA, and USDA should help lower costs and make commercialization possible. FAA officials added that more time, continued funding, and political support will help them achieve their goals.

- **Uncertainties inherent in new fuels technologies**. According to FAA officials, part of the underlying challenge of developing a sustainable supply chain is the limited financial investment by private industry due, in part, to risk associated with uncertainties. Such uncertainties include the ability of alternative fuels to compete with petroleum and the effects of possible future regulatory changes, such as the sustainability of tax credits, grants, or loan guarantees that support the development and commercialization of alternative jet fuel, factors which are not under FAA's authority.

- **Collaboration with many stakeholders**. Three subcommittee members identified challenges related to the need to collaborate with many stakeholders on this recommendation. For example, a subcommittee member also noted the need to collaborate with non-aviation stakeholders, such as agriculture-financing representatives, while two other members highlighted that work on this recommendation is a multi-agency process.

We recently began work in this area examining the progress made in developing alternative jet fuels in the United States, as well as the key challenges that exist and federal efforts that should be taken to address those challenges. We plan to report the results of our work in 2014.

Related Products

Biofuels: Potential Effects and Challenges of Required Increases in Production and Use. GAO-09-446. Washington, D.C.: August 25, 2009.

Aviation and Climate Change: Aircraft Emissions Expected to Grow, but Technological and Operational Improvements and Government Policies Can Help Control Emissions. GAO-09-554. Washington, D.C.: June 8, 2009.

*Aviation and the Environment: NextGen and Research and Development
Are Keys to Reducing Emissions and Their Impact on Health and
Climate.* GAO-08-706T. Washington, D.C.: May 6, 2008.

2. FAAC Recommendation— Harmonized Approach to CO_2 Reduction

Issue Overview

As previously noted, commercial aviation's contribution to greenhouse gas emissions is reported to be relatively small, but is forecasted to grow, with carbon dioxide (CO_2) emissions being the most significant greenhouse gas.[4] The 1997 Kyoto Protocol, an international agreement to minimize the adverse effects of climate change, stated that greenhouse gases from aviation fuels should be limited or reduced, and that such efforts should be conducted through ICAO.[5] In 2010, the ICAO Assembly agreed upon the following goals:

- achieve a global annual average fuel efficiency improvement rate of 2 percent until 2020 and pursue an aspirational global fuel efficiency improvement rate of 2 percent per year from 2021 to 2050; and
- achieve global carbon-neutral growth from 2020 onward.[6]

The United States and two airline industry groups—the International Air Transportation Association and Airlines for America—also established greenhouse-gas emission reduction goals. In line with the ICAO goals, FAA adopted a goal improving the National Airspace System's energy efficiency by at least 2 percent per year, and a goal of achieving carbon neutral growth by 2020 using a baseline of 2005. The industry groups agreed to a goal of improving fuel efficiency by 1.5 percent per year, rather than 2 percent, and achieving carbon-neutral growth from 2020,

---

[4]GAO, *Aviation and Climate Change: Aircraft Emissions Expected to Grow, but Technological and Operational Improvements and Government Policies Can Help Control Emissions,* GAO-09-554 (Washington, D.C.: June 8, 2009).

[5]ICAO is an advisory organization affiliated with the United Nations that aims to promote the establishment of international civil aviation standards and recommended practices and procedures.

[6]In subsequent meetings, ICAO's Committee on Aviation Environmental Protection also agreed on a metric to characterize aircraft CO_2 emissions and aircraft emissions certification procedures.

and set another explicit goal to halve CO_2 emissions by 2050 relative to 2005 levels.

However, the European Union (EU) took unilateral steps on this issue by including aviation in the EU Emissions Trading Scheme (ETS), a cap-and-trade system. Under ETS, the EU places a cap on emissions and requires airlines to secure allowances to emit greenhouse gasses. The EU provides most of the allowances at no charge, but sells about 15 percent of the allowances to the airlines. ETS was to be applied to flights arriving or departing at an EU airport, including those arriving from and departing to non-EU ETS countries, beginning in January 2012, but those efforts have been delayed. In April 2013, the EU approved a one-year suspension. Under the terms of the suspension, ETS continues to apply to all flights that depart and land in an EU country, but does not apply to flights that depart to or arrive from another region. The EU is awaiting action by ICAO to determine its next steps.

Given that the large U.S. commercial airlines serve a global network, the FAAC raised concerns on the number of proposals for taxes, emissions trading, and other methods intended to constrain emissions, noting that overlapping and conflicting proposals could hinder progress and siphon funds from industry investments in effective emissions reduction methods. For example, in addition to the EU ETS, according to the FAAC report, some countries also have their own environmental fees on airline activities.

DOT's and FAA's Actions to Address Recommendation

Table 5 provides a summary of the FAAC recommendation to establish a harmonized framework for CO_2 reductions and DOT's and FAA's actions to address it, as of June 2013.

Table 5: FAAC Recommendation on Establishing a Harmonized Framework for Aviation CO_2 Reductions and DOT's and FAA's Actions to Address It, as of June 2013

FAAC recommendation—emission reduction	DOT/FAA actions
Lead an effort to align Federal aviation policy to support an aviation sector approach to carbon emissions by specifically: • Building on the International Civil Aviation Organization (ICAO) resolution adopted on October 8, 2010, advocate for a coordinated global and domestic framework for aviation CO_2 emissions. • Taking advantage of industry assets to develop practical global implementation methods.	FAA officials stated they engaged with other agencies and industry to establish a domestic approach to reducing CO_2 emissions and participate in ICAO's efforts to establish an international consensus on CO_2 reduction goals. According to FAA officials, while these discussions preceded the issuance of the FAAC report in April 2011, the effort to establish a framework to reduce emissions is an ongoing process. The officials said that the European Union's (EU) Emissions Trading Scheme (ETS) and other unilateral efforts to curb emissions helped galvanize efforts to reach consensus at ICAO. FAA and DOT publicly opposed the ETS in favor of multilateral discussions at ICAO. Congress reaffirmed this position in the FAA Modernization and Reform Act of 2012 passed in February 2012[a] and in the European Union Emissions Trading Scheme Prohibition Act of 2011.[b] Partially as a result of this opposition, the EU approved a one-year suspension of ETS in April 2013 for flights between countries participating in EU ETS and countries that are not. To meet the October 2011 goals agreed upon through ICAO, FAA—working with other federal agencies and the aviation industry—developed an Aviation Environmental and Energy Policy Statement (Policy Statement) as well as an Aviation Greenhouse Gas Emissions Reduction Plan (Reduction Plan). The Reduction Plan describes how FAA, other federal agencies, and the industry will meet these goals: • improve flight operations with NextGen[c] • improve aircraft and engine technology; • support the development and deployment of alternative fuels; • develop policy mechanisms to supplement efforts on technology, operations and fuels; and • conduct research into the environmental impacts of aviations emissions. This approach is generally consistent with what aviation experts told us in 2009—that is, operational improvements stemming from NextGen, such as more direct plane routing, and research and development of engine and aircraft technologies will help reduce greenhouse gas emissions in the aviation sector.[d]

Source: FAAC report and GAO analysis of FAA documents and interviews.

[a]Pub. L. No. 112-95, § 509, 126 Stat. 11, 106-107.

[b]Pub. L. No. 112-200, §§ 2, 3, 126 Stat 1477, 1478 (2012).

[e]FAA, in collaboration with other federal agencies and the aviation industry, is transforming the nation's ground-based air-traffic control system to an air-traffic management system using satellite-based navigation and other technology. This transformation is referred to as NextGen. GAO has noted that NextGen, if implemented effectively, can help reduce aviation emissions by allowing for more direct routing, which could improve fuel efficiency and reduce carbon dioxide emission. Additional information on NextGen can be found in this report, in the discussion of recommendation 4.

[d]GAO, *Aviation and Climate Change: Aircraft Emissions Expected to Grow, but Technological and Operational Improvements and Government Policies Can Help Control Emissions*, GAO-09-554 (Washington, D.C.: June 8, 2009).

DOT's and FAA's Planned Actions	FAA officials stated that addressing this recommendation is a long-term effort and noted their ongoing efforts in this area. For example, FAA officials noted that continued domestic and international coordination are required to address this recommendation. FAA officials said implementing its Reduction Plan will continue to require sustained collaboration with partner agencies such as the National Aeronautics and Space Administration and the aviation industry. FAA officials said they would advocate that countries' reduction plans be updated on a triennial basis and would plan to update the U.S. Reduction Plan in 2015 and triennially afterward, if requested by future ICAO agreements. Officials also told us that they will participate in discussions on market-based measures at the upcoming ICAO Assembly meeting in September 2013.[7]
FAAC Members' Assessment of DOT's and FAA's Progress	All five of the FAAC environmental subcommittee members told us that the recommendation was not fully addressed, noting that work in this area was ongoing and that FAA should continue their involvement in ICAO's ongoing efforts.
Challenges in Implementing the Recommendation	• **Obtaining stakeholder consensus**. GAO previously found that it is important to coordinate when dealing with a global aviation network.[8] FAA officials and FAAC subcommittee members noted that an inherent challenge with this recommendation is the need to obtain consensus among an array of stakeholders, such as other federal agencies, industry stakeholders, and the many countries participating in ICAO. FAA officials recognized the threat of unilateral proposals to reduce aviation emissions via a market-based mechanism, such as the ETS, as a challenge to obtaining a harmonized approach. In addition, one subcommittee member raised concerns about FAA's and the industry's ability to meet FAA's more stringent goal for carbon-neutral growth using 2005 as the baseline year versus ICAO and industry goals that use 2020 as the baseline year. FAA officials have acknowledged that industry was concerned with the 2005

[7]Market-based measures can establish a price for emissions and provide incentives to airlines and consumers to reduce emissions. Examples include a cap-and-trade system or a tax on emissions.

[8]GAO, *Next Generation Air Transportation: Collaborative Efforts with European Union Generally Mirror Effective Practices, but Near-Term Challenges Could Delay Implementation*, GAO-12-48 (Washington, D.C.: Nov. 3, 2011).

baseline, but said that they have adopted this goal because it is consistent with the U.S. government's commitment made during the 2009 round of U.N. negotiations on climate change (the Copenhagen Accord) and reflects the position that the United States, Mexico, and Canada jointly took prior to the ICAO Assembly meeting in 2010.

- **Resource constraints**. FAA officials and a FAAC member told us that sustained federal financial support will be necessary to achieve the technical and operational improvements that are expected to result in emissions reductions consistent with ICAO and FAA goals. For example, resource constraints at the agency could hamper efforts to implement NextGen within the expected time frames; conduct necessary research and development of new technologies, including sustainable alternative jet fuels; and participate in the work and discussions at ICAO and other forums.

Related Products

NextGen Air Transportation System: FAA Has Made Some Progress in Midterm Implementation, but Ongoing Challenges Limit Expected Benefits. GAO-13-264. Washington, D.C.: April 8, 2013.

Aviation and Climate Change: Aircraft Emissions Expected to Grow, but Technological and Operational Improvements and Government Policies Can Help Control Emissions. GAO-09-554. Washington, D.C.: June 8, 2009.

International Climate Change Programs: Lessons Learned from the European Union's Emissions Trading Scheme and the Kyoto Protocol's Clean Development Mechanism. GAO-09-151. Washington, D.C.: November 18, 2008.

Aviation and the Environment: NextGen and Research and Development Are Keys to Reducing Emissions and Their Impact on Health and Climate. GAO-08-706T. Washington, D.C.: May 6, 2008.

Aviation and the Environment: Strategic Framework Needed to Address Challenges Posed by Aircraft Emissions. GAO-03-252. Washington, D.C.: February 28, 2003.

3. FAAC Recommendation—Support Extending the Alternative Minimum Tax Exemption

Issue Overview

Municipal bond proceeds are a significant funding source for airports' capital development.[9] Municipal bonds for airports are generally classified as private activity bonds, since the bond proceeds are used for private business purposes. The private activity bonds for airports are tax-exempt (also known as "qualified" private activity bonds).[10] However, qualified private activity bonds are subject to restrictions that do not apply to governmental bonds. Among these restrictions, the interest income from qualified private activity bonds is included in income when calculating the alternative minimum tax (AMT), whereas the interest on governmental bonds is not.[11] A bondholder whose total income reached the level subject to the AMT would have to pay tax on the interest earned from airport qualified private activity bonds.

The FAAC argued that investors in these bonds demand an interest rate premium to compensate for the AMT tax liability, which can raise the costs of airport projects. The American Recovery and Reinvestment Act of 2009 exempted new issuances of all private activity bonds from the

---

[9]See GAO, *Airport Finance: Observations on Planned Airport Development Costs and Funding Levels and the Administration's Proposed Changes in the Airport Improvement Program*, GAO-07-885 (Washington, D.C.: June 29, 2007).

[10]The interest earned on most bonds issued by state and local governments is tax-exempt, meaning that the interest paid to bondholders is generally not included in their gross income for federal income tax purposes. Tax-exempt bonds reduce the issuer's borrowing costs because purchasers of such debt are willing to accept a lower rate of interest than that of taxable debt of comparable risk and maturity.

[11]AMT is a separate federal tax system that applies to both individual and corporate taxpayers. It parallels the income tax system but with different rules for determining taxable income, different tax rates for computing tax liability, and different rules for allowing the use of tax credits.

AMT in 2009 and 2010, and allowed for the refinancing of some private activity bonds into non-AMT debt.[12]

DOT's and FAA's Actions to Address Recommendation

Table 6 provides a summary of the FAAC recommendation to support extending the AMT exemption and DOT's and FAA's actions to address it, as of June 2013.

Table 6: FAAC Recommendation on Extending the AMT Exemption for Private Activity Bonds and DOT's and FAA's Actions to Address It, as of June 2013

FAAC recommendation—AMT exemption	DOT/FAA actions
Support federal legislation to provide a 4-year extension of the alternative minimum tax (AMT) exemption for private activity bonds.	In May 2012, DOT sent a letter to Congress supporting adoption of the Moving Ahead for Progress in the 21st Century Act.[a] DOT specifically supported a provision of the bill that included support for extending the AMT exemption for all private activity bonds, including airport private-activity bonds; however, the AMT exemption was not included in the final legislation.

Source: FAAC report and GAO analysis of DOT and FAA documents and interviews.

[a]Adopted as the Moving Ahead for Progress in the 21st Century Act, Pub. L. No. 112-141, 126 Stat. 405 (2012).

DOT's and FAA's Planned Actions

FAA officials told us that any further action on extending the AMT exemption to private activity bonds would require legislative action, and there is not currently a legislative vehicle for this provision.[13] As a result, DOT does not plan to take any additional actions and considers the recommendation to be closed.

FAAC Members' Assessment of DOT's and FAA's Progress

While all six of the FAAC finance subcommittee members acknowledged that extending the AMT exemption requires legislation, five of the six stated that DOT should continue to work for passage of an AMT exemption for airport private activity bonds. Two subcommittee members stated that in their view, DOT should reach out to aviation and airport industry stakeholders to leverage their support for the exemption. One

---

[12] Pub. L. No. 111-5, § 1503, 123 Stat. 115, 354 (2009), amending 26 U.S.C. §§ 56, 57.

[13]In addition, the President's budget proposal for fiscal year 2014 includes provisions that may affect AMT exemptions, such as a proposal to limit the tax rate at which high income taxpayers can reduce their tax liability to a maximum of 28 percent.

subcommittee member did not think that an AMT exemption should be included in legislation without a cost-benefit analysis.

Challenges in Implementing the Recommendation

- **Mixed perspectives on the appropriateness of the AMT exemption**. FAA may face challenges encouraging congressional action on this recommendation due to mixed perspectives on the appropriateness of tax-exemptions for bond financing. Our prior work has shown the importance of determining the economic efficiency of applying preferential tax treatment to selected investments.[14] High-level analyses of the AMT exemption have shown it leads to a loss of federal revenue, but data specific to airports is limited.[15] However, FAA and industry stakeholders counter that exempting airport private activity bonds has led to significant savings. FAA conducted an analysis of the financial impact of the AMT exemption in the American Recovery and Reinvestment Act of 2009, and stated that the exemption resulted in significant savings for airports, increased capital investment, and increased employment. Our tax expenditure guide provides useful resources for evaluating the efficiency of applying preferential tax treatment to selected investments, and could assist Congress as it considers these provisions.[16]

- **Legislative change**. As previously noted, any further action on extending the AMT exemption to private activity bonds will require legislative action. One FAAC subcommittee member noted that airport stakeholders may face challenges in lobbying for such an exemption given their limited financial resources and lack of natural alliances with other industries that previously received an exemption from the AMT.

---

[14]GAO, *Tax Expenditures: Background and Evaluation Criteria and Questions*, GAO-13-167SP (Washington, D.C.: Nov. 29, 2012).

[15]The Joint Committee on Taxation estimated that temporarily exempting all private activity bonds from the AMT for 2012 would have reduced federal revenue by $215 million over the 10-year period from 2012 through 2022. In addition, the Congressional Budget Office and the Joint Committee on Taxation issued a joint report in 2009 which found that tax-exempt bonds are a costly and inefficient method for delivering a subsidy, because the loss of federal receipts is greater than the reduction in the interest costs of tax-exempt issuers.

[16]GAO-13-167SP.

Related Products

Tax Expenditures: Background and Evaluation Criteria and Questions. GAO-13-167SP. Washington, D.C.: November 29, 2012.

Tax Policy: Tax-Exempt Status of Certain Bonds Merits Reconsideration, and Apparent Noncompliance with Issuance Cost Limitations Should Be Addressed. GAO-08-364. Washington, D.C.: February 15, 2008.

Airport Finance: Observations on Planned Airport Development Costs and Funding Levels and the Administration's Proposed Changes in the Airport Improvement Program. GAO-07-885. Washington, D.C.: June 29, 2007.

4. FAAC Recommendation— Funding Accelerated NextGen Equipage of Aircraft

Issue Overview

FAA is transforming the nation's ground-based air-traffic control system to an air-traffic management system using satellite-based navigation and other technology. This transformation is referred to as NextGen. NextGen is intended to enhance airspace safety, reduce delays, save fuel, and reduce carbon dioxide emissions and other adverse environmental impacts.

While some operational improvements can be made with existing aircraft equipment, realizing more significant benefits of NextGen necessitates additional investment by airlines in new technologies to establish a critical mass of properly equipped aircraft.[17] However, GAO and others have noted that a variety of disincentives may deter operators from investing early in NextGen equipment. For example, we have reported that aircraft operators may be hesitant to make investments in equipment if they do not have confidence that FAA will deliver the systems, procedures, and capabilities to realize the benefits from their investments.[18] In addition, the FAAC report identified challenges for FAA to overcome in encouraging operators to equip early, including: (1) prior instances in which operators equipped aircraft but received little or no benefit because the FAA did not implement quickly enough the necessary procedures or approvals to enable operators to derive benefits from the equipment; and (2) the business case may be weak for individual operators to purchase and install equipment early, with costs far exceeding expected direct benefits to users.

---

[17]In April 2013, we reported on FAA's efforts to deliver benefits in the midterm (through 2018) by implementing operational improvements that use available technologies. See GAO, *NextGen Air Transportation System: FAA Has Made Some Progress in Midterm Implementation, but Ongoing Challenges Limit Expected Benefits*, GAO-13-264 (Washington, D.C.: Apr. 8, 2013).

[18]GAO, *Next Generation Air Transportation System: FAA Faces Implementation Challenges*, GAO-12-1011T (Washington, D.C.: Sept. 12, 2012).

The FAAC noted that accelerated deployment of NextGen could lead to capacity, efficiency, environmental, and safety benefits. It also emphasized the need to overcome challenges in encouraging operators to equip early by providing some form of public financing to incentivize equipage. One FAAC finance subcommittee member formally dissented to this recommendation and questioned the need for public financing of airline equipment, citing a lack of evidence that the benefits gained from equipment investments would not be sufficient to encourage industry adoption without government subsidies.

DOT's and FAA's Actions to Address Recommendation

Table 7 provides a summary of the FAAC recommendation to accelerate investment and installation of NextGen equipment on aircraft and FAA's actions to address it, as of June 2013.

Table 7: FAAC Recommendation on Accelerating NextGen Equipage and DOT's and FAA's Actions to Address It, as of June 2013

FAAC recommendation—accelerated equipage	DOT/FAA actions
Undertake a significant financial investment to achieve extensive public benefits through the accelerated equipage of commercial and general aviation aircraft with NextGen equipment and technologies.	At the request of FAA, in September 2011, the NextGen Advisory Committee (NAC)[a] recommended specific avionics required to achieve NextGen midterm capability goals, as well as the types of operational benefits necessary to incentivize operators to further invest in these avionics. In February 2012, FAA received authority through the FAA Modernization and Reform Act to establish a program to facilitate public-private financing for equipping commercial- and general-aviation aircraft with NextGen technologies.[b]
• The federal commitment must be matched in some fashion by financial or operational commitments—for example reduced carbon dioxide emission on the part of aviation operators.	
• This public-private partnership should focus on equipping aircraft and training staff to use key NextGen technology and operational capabilities including Performance-Based Navigation (PBN), Automatic Dependent Surveillance-Broadcast (ADS-B), Ground-Based Augmentation System, and Data Communications.	FAA is in the process of determining how to structure a financial incentive program that would encourage deployment of NextGen-capable aircraft sooner than would have occurred without such funding assistance in place. Since FAA does not have funding for the incentive program and the statute directed FAA to maximize private sector capital, FAA officials said that they reached out to other federal agencies, such as the Departments of Agriculture, Education, Energy, and the modal administrations of Transportation to understand various options for establishing a loan-guarantee program. Based on the NAC's recommendations, FAA proposed two avionics equipage bundles focused on operators: one for air carriers flying in the busiest metroplexes and one for operators that fly elsewhere. Each equipage bundle identified minimum and operational equipment. FAA then conducted outreach through public meetings, market surveys, and individual meetings with aviation representatives to get industry perspectives on the overall program structure and the proposed equipage bundles.
• A menu of financial options—grants, loans, leases, and loan guarantees—should be designed in consultation with industry, and this financing could be managed through an infrastructure bank or other financing vehicle. The form and structure of the financial options offered depend on the appropriateness of the incentive for the technology and capability being funded, the aviation operators involved, the costs and benefits associated with the particular technology or operational capability, and the shared responsibility between the public and private partners. An important part of this program will be the detailing of commitments that both the FAA and operators should make to deliver promised benefits or mitigate financial or other risk.	FAA officials noted that the efforts to establish a financial incentive program is one piece in a broader effort to develop incentives for aircraft operators. FAA has also noted the need to demonstrate the benefits of NextGen equipment, which would help create a business case for operators to equip early.[c] For example, FAA has entered into agreements with JetBlue, UPS, and United Airlines to provide or upgrade equipment and obtain ADS-B data to validate the business case for early adoption of ADS-B.[d] FAA officials stated that these ADS-B data will help the agency measure operational benefits, reduce uncertainty, and help to determine time frames for the carriers to obtain a return on their investment. In addition, FAA's Data Communications (DataComm) contract includes an incentives goal to equip 1,900 aircraft to create a critical mass of equipped aircraft and demonstrate the benefits of equipping with this technology.[e]

Source: FAAC report and GAO analysis of DOT and FAA documents and interviews.

[a]The NAC is comprised of aviation stakeholders from the government and industry. The NAC was set up by RTCA at the request of FAA, and is the follow-on to RTCA's Air Traffic Management Advisory Committee. The NAC working group seeks to develop a common understanding of priorities in the context of overall NextGen capabilities and implementation constraints, with an emphasis on improvements through 2018. The committee primarily focuses on implementation issues, including

prioritization criteria at a national level, joint investment priorities, and location and timing of capability implementation.

[b]Pub. L. No. 112-95, § 221(a), 126 Stat. 11, 53.

[c]FAA's current NextGen implementation plans includes midterm implementation activities through 2020 and the long term to 2025 and beyond.

[d]ADS-B is a surveillance technology that, in part, enables aircraft to continually broadcast flight data, such as position, air speed, and altitude, among other types of information, to air traffic controllers and other aircraft for more precise tracking of aircraft.

[e]DataComm is a next generation data communications system that is intended to provide a digital communications link for two-way data exchanges between controllers and flight crews.

DOT's and FAA's Planned Actions

FAA officials stated FAA has addressed this recommendation, with the help of the authority granted in the FAA Modernization and Reform Act. Officials noted that they are still working to determine what the program will entail, including soliciting input from aircraft operators and potential private partners to determine how to establish an incentive program that operators want to participate in. In addition, the appropriations requirements for a loan guarantee program has not yet been met.[19] FAA officials also noted that they are considering how to administer the loan guarantee program and FAA may need to issue a contract for an external group to fulfill this role; however, FAA currently does not have funding to do so.

FAAC Members' Assessment of DOT's and FAA's Progress

Five of the six finance FAAC subcommittee members stated that the recommendation was not fully addressed, although one subcommittee member did not agree with the recommendation, as noted earlier. The remaining subcommittee member said FAA had addressed the recommendation, but noted that it still needed legislative authority to issue loan guarantees. Of the five subcommittee members who said it was not fully addressed, two members stated that FAA is taking steps to address the recommendation. Two other members stated that FAA should take additional steps to collaborate with industry to design an incentive program and develop a stronger business case for airlines to invest in equipping early. These two subcommittee members felt that FAA should conduct additional outreach on these issues, with one stating that FAA should have reached out to industry to discuss various incentive options prior to taking steps to create a loan-guarantee program. FAA

---

[19]See Federal Credit Reform Act of 1990, Pub. L. No. 93–344, § 504, as added by Pub. L. No. 101–508, 104 Stat. 1388–609 (1990), codified at 2 U.S.C. § 661c(b).

officials noted that while they have been focused on possibly establishing a loan guarantee program given the mandate to maximize private investment and a lack of funding for a different type of program, they have solicited input from industry on ideas for other incentive programs that would maximize private investment and have not received any specific suggestions.

Challenges in Implementing the Recommendation	• **Demonstrating benefits to encourage industry participation**. FAA officials and two FAAC members noted that beyond providing financial incentives, demonstrating operational benefits is key to encouraging early equipage by operators. However, FAA officials explained that the extent to which a new capability or procedure provides an operational benefit will vary among carriers. For example, if a new procedure is deployed in airspace where a carrier is not operating, the carrier will not receive a benefit from early equipage. FAA officials noted they are working to address this challenge by asking operators—through market surveys, as well as public and private meetings—whether providing certain services in certain locations would encourage operators to invest in equipment earlier. However, FAA officials told us they have generally faced difficulties in collecting specific information on which capabilities and locations specific operators would be interested in.
	• **Reducing uncertainty with NextGen time frames**. We have found that stakeholders are concerned that FAA has not made sufficient progress in deploying systems and producing benefits. For example, a past FAA program's cancellation contributed to skepticism about FAA's commitment to follow through with its plans.[20] Two FAAC subcommittee members noted that FAA's timely installment of infrastructure, including equipment at airports and FAA facilities, is essential to realizing NextGen benefits. Along those same lines, another FAAC subcommittee member noted that FAA needs to make a business case for airlines to invest within time frames that FAA can deliver on the benefits so that the equipment does not become obsolete. Three subcommittee members also noted that uncertainty regarding NextGen time frames would pose a challenge to convincing

---

[20]GAO, *Next Generation Air Transportation System: Progress and Challenges Associated with the Transformation of the National Airspace System*, GAO-07-25 (Washington, D.C.: Nov. 13, 2006).

operators to equip, with two subcommittee members noting that sequestration[21] has introduced an additional level of uncertainty into NextGen implementation time frames. In April 2013, we noted that stakeholders, including RTCA and the NextGen Advisory Committee, have stressed the need for additional information to understand the potential direct costs, benefits, and return on investments that might be realized from technological and equipage investments.[22] While FAA's NextGen plans include some examples of benefits, RTCA reported in 2011 that available FAA plans do not include sufficient information for airlines making investment decisions such as forecast benefits by either location or usage, or the proportion of the local fleet that is currently equipped.[23,24] We noted that without greater certainty on when and where NextGen improvements are planned, airlines and others are unlikely to invest in the equipment, staffing, and training needed to help achieve the full benefits of NextGen implementation. We recommended FAA assure that NextGen planning documents provide stakeholders information on how and when operational improvements are expected to achieve NextGen goals and targets.[25] In June 2013, DOT concurred with our recommendation and stated that it has efforts underway to better integrate various NextGen plans to provide more of this type of information.

---

[21]The Balanced Budget and Emergency Deficit Control Act (BBEDCA), as amended, established discretionary spending limits for fiscal years 2012 to 2021. 2 U.S.C. § 901. BBEDCA also required the Office of Management and Budget to calculate, and the President to order, a sequestration, i.e., cancellation, of budgetary resources on March 1, 2013. *See* 2 U.S.C. § 901a. For fiscal year 2013, the President ordered a sequestration of about $85 billion. *Sequestration Order for Fiscal Year 2013 Pursuant to Section 251A of the Balanced Budget and Emergency Deficit Control Act, As Amended*, 78 Fed. Reg. 14633 (Mar. 6, 2013).

[22]GAO-13-264. Organized in 1935, RTCA (once known as Radio Technical Commission for Aeronautics) is a private, not-for-profit corporation that develops consensus-based recommendations for communications, navigation, surveillance, and air traffic management system issues.

[23]RTCA, *NextGen Equipage: User Business Case Gaps, A Report of the NextGen Advisory Committee in Response to Tasking from the Federal Aviation Administration* (September 2011).

[24]Information about the level of local equipage is important because the level of equipage can affect how often airlines are able to use new routes. A new route into Chicago, for example, that allows for the simultaneous use of runways at O'Hare International and Midway has to be closed whenever a non-equipped aircraft arrives on the approach to Midway.

[25]GAO-13-264.

Related Products

NextGen Air Transportation System: FAA Has Made Some Progress in Midterm Implementation, but Ongoing Challenges Limit Expected Benefits. GAO-13-264. Washington, D.C.: April 8, 2013.

Next Generation Air Transportation System: FAA Faces Implementation Challenges. GAO-12-1011T. Washington, D.C.: September 12, 2012.

Next Generation Air Transportation System: FAA Has Made Some Progress in Implementation, but Delays Threaten to Impact Costs and Benefits. GAO-12-141T. Washington, D.C.: October 5, 2011.

Next Generation Air Transportation System: Challenges with Partner Agency and FAA Coordination Continue, and Efforts to Integrate Near-, Mid-, and Long-term Activities Are Ongoing. GAO-10-649T. Washington, D.C.: April 21, 2010.

Next Generation Air Transportation System: FAA Faces Challenges in Responding to Task Force Recommendations. GAO-10-188T. Washington, D.C.: October 28, 2009.

Next Generation Air Transportation System: Progress and Challenges Associated with the Transformation of the National Airspace System. GAO-07-25. Washington, D.C.: November 13, 2006.

5. FAAC Recommendation— Review Criteria for the Airport Improvement Program and Passenger Facility Charge Program Related to NextGen

Issue Overview

The Airport Improvement Program (AIP) and Passenger Facility Charge (PFC) Program provide airports with funding for airport development and planning projects.[26] Under AIP, FAA may provide eligible airports with grants,[27] using funds drawn from the Airport and Airway Trust Fund,[28] for projects related to planning, development, or noise-compatibility projects. In general, airports can use AIP funds on most airfield capital improvements, such as new runways or runway lengthening, or repairs and in some specific situations, for terminals, hangars, and non-aviation development.[29] The PFC program allows eligible airports to collect fees

---

[26]The AIP was established by the Airport and Airway Improvement Act of 1982 (Pub. L. No. 97-248, § 505, 96 Stat. 324, codified as positive law at 49 U.S.C. chapter 471), and the PFC was authorized under the Aviation Safety and Capacity Expansion Act of 1990 (Pub. L. No. 101-508, § 9110, 104 Stat. 1388-353, codified as positive law at 49 U.S.C, § 40117).

[27]To be eligible for AIP, an airport must be included in FAA's National Plan of Integrated Airport Systems, which identifies airports that are significant to national air transportation and contribute to the needs of civil aviation, national defense, and the Postal Service.

[28]The Airport and Airway Trust Fund is funded principally by a variety of excise taxes paid by users of the national airspace system, as well as by interest revenue. The excise taxes are imposed on airline ticket purchases and aviation fuel, as well as the shipment of cargo.

[29]Projects related to airport operations and revenue-generating improvements are typically not eligible for funding. For example, operational costs, such as salaries, equipment, and supplies, and commercial revenue-producing portions of airports and airport terminals are generally not eligible for AIP grants.

up to $4.50 for every boarded passenger at commercial airports.[30] Airports can use this funding for FAA-approved projects related to enhancing airport safety, capacity, security, noise compatibility, and for enhancing competition among airlines.[31] Project eligibility is almost identical between AIP and the PFC program except that airports may use PFC funding for repaying bonds and for airline waiting areas and gates that generally are not eligible for AIP grants because they are considered revenue producing for airlines.

In its report, the FAAC noted interest among the aviation community in broadening AIP and PFC eligibility criteria to support aviation infrastructure projects, including those related to NextGen—FAA's initiative to transform the nation's ground-based air-traffic control system to an air-traffic management system using satellite-based navigation and other advanced technology. However, the FAAC noted that current regulations do not generally allow AIP or PFC funds to be used for NextGen-related projects.

DOT's and FAA's Actions to Address Recommendation

Table 8 provides a summary of the FAAC recommendation to assess AIP and PFC eligibility criteria for NextGen projects and FAA's actions to address it, as of June 2013.

---

[30]PFCs are collected as part of the current ticket payment and distribution process, which involves many parties. Airlines remit PFCs to airports minus a small administrative charge per PFC collected. GAO, *Alternative Methods for Collecting Airport Passenger Facility Charges,* GAO-13-262R (Washington, D.C.: Feb. 14, 2013).

[31]According to a 2013 GAO report, most PFC funds, or 74 percent of approved collection revenue for PFC projects, are used to enhance capacity and reduce congestion. GAO-13-262R.

Table 8: FAAC Recommendation on Airport Improvement Program (AIP) and Passenger Facility Charge (PFC) Eligibility for NextGen Projects and DOT's and FAA's Actions to Address It, as of June 2013

FAAC recommendation—AIP and PFC	DOT/FAA actions
Review the eligibility criteria for AIP and PFC programs and consider whether investing AIP and PFC dollars in NextGen equipment, operational capabilities, and performance-based procedures is needed. If so, FAA should do as much as possible to administratively update the eligibility criteria and develop legislative recommendations to the Secretary of Transportation for the remainder of the suggested changes.	Prior to the FAAC recommendation, in September 2010, FAA created a working group tasked to review AIP and PFC funding eligibility for NextGen systems that would be beneficial to airports and also to make recommendations for expanded AIP eligibility through legislation or other means. This group identified several airport projects that were already being funded with AIP and PFC funds and assisted NextGen systems, such as clearing obstructions, which enable lower approaches for aircraft using NextGen technologies, and other airfield improvements, such as the installation of lighting and signs.[a]
	During the course of the working group's review, FAA issued a 2011 finding that allowed AIP grants to be used for the purchase of transponders ("squitters") for airport ground vehicles, such as snow plows, airport rescue and firefighting vehicles, and airside operations vehicles. Squitters emit a signal from the vehicles, which is tracked using NextGen surveillance technology, improving vehicle visibility and enhancing airport safety.[b] In fiscal year 2012, three airports applied and received grants, totaling $1,265,625, for this equipment. The working group also identified other NextGen-related projects that would require statutory changes before they could be eligible for AIP funding. For example, the group reviewed the use of sensors that rely on NextGen surveillance technology for airports located in mountainous areas where radars cannot track aircraft.[c] FAA officials said while the sensors are a low-cost investment that could improve capacity, they determined that funding such an investment with AIP would require legislative changes. According to FAA officials, the existing AIP authorizing statute does not allow AIP funding for surveillance technology that provides airborne aircraft tracking data for air traffic control services, such as multilateration technologies. In June 2013, DOT's website on the status of the FAAC recommendations stated that, for the next FAA authorization, FAA is considering recommending a pilot program to permit states to fund installation of ADS-B ground stations to provide airborne surveillance coverage.

Source: FAAC report and GAO analysis of DOT and FAA documents and interviews.

[a]Although our discussion with FAA officials focused on the AIP program, they noted that projects eligible under AIP would also be eligible under PFC.

[b]One of the programs under NextGen is the use of Automatic Dependent Surveillance-Broadcast (ADS-B), which includes a surveillance system where an aircraft or other vehicle uses a global navigation satellite system to determine and broadcast its position. Squitters are one type of ADS-B Out reporting units and can be used in the land-based vehicles, allowing them to broadcast their location to air traffic control and other suitably equipped vehicles.

[c]For example, in Colorado, mountainous terrain made installing traditional radar too expensive. Because of the lack of radar coverage, FAA limits the number of aircraft flying in the area. To address this issue, the Colorado Department of Transportation installed Wide Area Multilateration (WAM) stations, which rely on distributed sensors that would allow Denver's air traffic control center to determine an aircraft's position and allow a greater number of aircraft to fly in the area. While the Colorado Department of Transportation funded the installation of the radars because FAA determined that traditional radars were too expensive, FAA funded the installation of the sensors with support from FAA's Surveillance Broadcast Services office.

DOT's and FAA's Planned Actions	Although FAA officials told us they consider this recommendation addressed, they said that they continue to track other potential NextGen-related projects that could be recommended for funding through AIP and PFC. As noted in table 8, DOT's June 2013 update on the status of this recommendation stated that for the next FAA authorization, FAA is considering recommending a pilot program to permit states to fund installation of ADS-B ground stations to provide airborne surveillance coverage.
FAAC Members' Assessment of DOT's and FAA's Progress	Four of the six FAAC finance subcommittee members felt that the recommendation was not fully addressed. Of the two remaining subcommittee members, one did not feel that he had enough information about DOT's actions on the recommendation to determine whether it was fully addressed, while the other said that the recommendation with respect to AIP was addressed, but it was unclear what action DOT had taken with respect to the PFC program. Two of the subcommittee members, including one that did not provide an opinion on the status of the recommendation, stated that FAA's approach to the recommendation was very narrow and that the FAAC envisioned a broader review to determine how to expand the scope of the AIP and PFC programs. One of these subcommittee members stated FAA should have had additional meetings with airport representatives after the FAAC completed its work to explore options for rewriting the AIP and PFC program. Another subcommittee member stated that discussions related to AIP and PFC should reflect the context of the FAAC's recommendation to commission an independent study of federal aviation taxes and fees, which we did not examine as part of this report. Two subcommittee members noted the need to address funding issues, which are discussed in the challenges section.
Challenges in Implementing this Recommendation	• **Legislative change**. FAA officials told us that the challenge with implementing this recommendation is that extending eligibility for AIP and PFC funding often requires making changes to the authorizing statute. Two subcommittee members acknowledged this issue, but added that FAA should work with Congress to explore changing the programs. While during the course of our audit, FAA officials stated that they did not plan to recommend extending AIP and PFC eligibility to fund projects outside of traditional AIP projects because that funding is still needed by airports and NextGen has its own funding mechanism; as previously noted, DOT's June 2013 update stated that FAA is considering recommending legislation for a pilot program to

permit states to fund installation of ADS-B ground stations—a key
NextGen technology—which could potentially expand the use of PFC
funds.

- **Limited funding**. FAA officials and two subcommittee members
  stated that airports are struggling to address their immediate needs
  with the existing AIP and PFC funds, making it difficult to expand use
  of these funds to include NextGen projects. Appropriations for AIP
  have been flat—roughly $3.5 billion for fiscal years 2005 through
  2011—and are reduced under current authorized levels to be $3.35
  billion from fiscal year 2012 through fiscal year 2015. In addition, a
  recent statute allowed DOT to transfer funds from AIP to avoid air
  traffic controllers' furloughs and reduce the impacts of other
  reductions.[32] With respect to PFC, two subcommittee members noted
  that the PFC has not been increased. (The PFC has remained capped
  at $4.50 since 2000.)[33] As we have noted, airports have long sought
  to increase the PFC cap, arguing that the fee cap has not been
  adjusted for inflation, while airlines counter that raising the PFC
  inhibits demand for air travel.[34] One subcommittee member stated
  that expanding AIP and PFC eligibility to include additional costs
  would require a significant study to determine the most appropriate
  use of the funds.

Related Products

*Transportation: Alternative Methods for Collecting Airport Passenger
Facility Charges*. GAO-13-262R. Washington, D.C.: February 14, 2013.

*Airport Noise Grants: FAA Needs to Better Ensure Project Eligibility and
Improve Strategic Goal and Performance Measures*. GAO-12-890.
Washington, D.C.: September 12, 2012.

*Airport Finance: Observations on Planned Airport Development Costs
and Funding Levels and the Administration's Proposed Changes in the*

---

[32]Reducing Flight Delays Act of 2013, Pub. L. No. 113-9, § 2, 127 Stat. 443, 444 (2013).

[33]The President's Fiscal Year 2014 budget submission includes a proposal to raise the
PFC cap from $4.50 to $8.00 and lower AIP funding to $2.9 billion, offset in part by
eliminating passenger and cargo entitlement funding for large hub airports. This proposal
also would allow all commercial service airports to increase their non-federal passenger
facility charge.

[34]GAO-13-262R.

Airport Improvement Program. GAO-07-885. Washington, D.C.: June 29, 2007.

6. FAAC Recommendation— Promote Global Competitiveness

Issue Overview

Ongoing growth in the demand for international air travel presents opportunities for expansion for U.S. carriers. However, we previously found that U.S. carriers' ability to establish new routes can be limited by the policies of foreign governments.[35] Preferential treatment of national airlines restricts U.S. carriers' access to possibly large international markets. Other impediments to entry to foreign markets include barriers, such as slot restrictions, that limit the potential for service by U.S. carriers.[36]

DOT has taken steps to address restrictive market access policies. In 1992, DOT launched an initiative to enter into new "Open Skies" agreements with foreign countries. Open Skies agreements remove the vast majority of restrictions on how airlines of the two signatory countries may operate between and beyond their respective territories. For example, these agreements remove prohibitions on the routes that airlines of the signatory countries can fly or the number of airlines that can fly them. Open Skies agreements also provide underlying traffic rights and provisions for cooperative marketing arrangements that allow airlines from different countries to form alliances with one another. Operating in an alliance allows an airline to greatly expand its service network, without having to increase the number of routes it flies using its own aircraft. U.S.

---

[35]GAO, *Transatlantic Aviation: Effects of Easing Restrictions on U.S.-European Markets*, GAO-04-835 (Washington, D.C.: July 21, 2004). For decades, international air service has been governed by aviation agreements negotiated between countries to specify "traffic rights," such as the number of airlines that can operate between markets, the airports from and to which they operate, the number of flights that can be provided, and the fares that airlines could charge.

[36]Airport slots refer to the permission to land or take-off at a congested airport at a specific time on a specific day, and are also used at certain airports in the United States, such as three in New York and New Jersey. We reported on FAA's administration of slot restrictions. See, GAO, *Slot-Controlled Airports: FAA's Rules Could be Improved to Enhance Competition and Use of Available Capacity*, GAO-12-902 (Washington, D.C.: Sept. 13, 2012).

and foreign air carriers wishing to enter into an alliance may also request that DOT grant them immunity from the U.S. antitrust laws.[37] Antitrust immunity allows these airlines to coordinate their fares, services, and capacity as if they were a single carrier in these markets, subject to certain conditions. As part of its antitrust immunity review, DOT determines the effects of the immunized alliance on competition and whether the alliance serves the public interest. However, there is not universal agreement that alliances best serve the traveling public.[38]

DOT issued a 1995 Statement of U.S. International Air Transportation Policy recognizing the importance of international air service and the need to enable U.S. carriers to serve foreign markets. The policy provides a broad umbrella under which actions such as bilateral negotiations and antitrust immunity alliance reviews are taken and emphasized a number of objectives, including, but not limited to:

- providing carriers with unrestricted opportunities to develop services and systems to meet market demand;
- eliminating market distortions internationally, such as government subsidies and unequal access to infrastructure; and,
- encouraging the development of a cost-effective and productive air-transportation industry through addressing infrastructure needs, privatizing airlines, and reducing barriers to the creation of global aviation systems, such as limitations on cross-border investment, wherever possible.[39]

---

[37]49 U.S.C § 41308.

[38]Economists in the Department of Justice's Economic Analysis Group published a review of DOT's prior decisions to grant antitrust immunity for alliance requests and found that a grant of antitrust immunity to carriers in an alliance reduces competition in routes where these carriers offer competing flights and that fares paid by passengers for travel in non-stop trans-Atlantic flights are higher in routes with fewer independent competitors. The review's authors also stated that the data show that alliances can produce pricing efficiencies for trans-Atlantic passengers who travel with connecting itineraries, but antitrust immunity within an alliance is not necessary to achieve such efficiencies. Gillespie, William and Oliver M. Richard, *Antitrust Immunity and International Airline Alliances*, EAG 11-1 (February 2011), accessed April 11, 2013, http://www.justice.gov/atr/public/eag/267513.htm.

[39]Many countries limit foreign ownership of national airlines. For example, non-US citizens may not own more than 25 percent of the controlling interest in an American airline (or 50 percent of an equity interest).

The Secretary of Transportation also serves as a member of the President's Export Promotion Cabinet.[40] This cabinet was established through executive order in 2010 and was tasked with implementing the National Export Initiative, which seeks to double the dollar value of U.S. exports by the end of 2014.

The FAAC report applauded DOT's efforts to open foreign markets to U.S. airlines, but also noted that some of the world's fastest-growing aviation markets—including those in Asia, South America, and the Near East—remain restricted to U.S. air carriers. In addition, the FAAC noted that in some key markets, U.S. passenger and cargo air carriers not only face restrictive aviation agreements, but also must confront a wide range of practical market access barriers—including slot restrictions, airspace limitations, and local ground-handling rules—that increase their operating costs and limit U.S. air carriers' ability to compete, both domestically and globally. In addition, while many different factors can be included in DOT's public interest analysis of antitrust immunity for alliances, including wages and working conditions, some FAAC members expressed concerns on the impacts of immunized alliances between U.S. and foreign carriers on U.S. workers.

DOT's and FAA's Actions to Address Recommendation

DOT officials told us that their actions on this recommendation consisted of a three-prong approach: (1) fostering conditions that enable global alliances to develop as well as ensuring DOT gives weight to existing statutory criteria when reviewing requests for antitrust immunity for alliances between U.S. and foreign carriers; (2) continuing efforts to open foreign markets to U.S. carriers; and (3) expanding DOT's role in promoting aviation exports. Table 9 provides a summary of the FAAC recommendation to promote global competitiveness and DOT's actions to address it, as of June 2013.

---

[40]The Export Promotion Cabinet consists of the Secretaries of State, Treasury, Agriculture, Commerce, Labor, Energy, and Transportation; the Director of the Office of Management and Budget; the United States Trade Representative; the Assistant to the President for Economic Policy; the National Security Advisor; the Chair of the Council of Economic Advisers; the President of the Export-Import Bank of the United States; the Administrator of the Small Business Administration; the President of the Overseas Private Investment Corporation; and the Director of the United States Trade and Development Agency.

Table 9: FAAC Recommendation on Promoting Global Competitiveness and DOT's and FAA's Actions to Address It, as of June 2013

FAAC recommendation—global competitiveness	DOT/FAA actions
Foster conditions that enable global air carrier alliances that enhance the viability and global competitiveness of U.S. air carriers, airports, and manufacturers, and protect and create U.S. aviation industry jobs by reaffirming the general objectives of the Department of Transportation's 1995 Statement of U.S. International Air Transportation Policy (the 1995 Statement).[a]	DOT officials noted that, because the 1995 statement remains applicable today, it was not necessary to reaffirm it. DOT officials added that they worked to foster conditions that enable global alliances by working with foreign regulatory authorities to discuss industry trends or specific transactions, such as an application for antitrust immunity. DOT officials noted that they meet periodically with other regulators to share information on cases and cooperate on alliance monitoring efforts. DOT also stated that they had established a dialogue with stakeholders to facilitate the exchange of information on any impediments to the implementation of alliances around the world.
Ensure that, as the DOT performs its public interest analysis, it gives substantial weight to existing statutory criteria that would help ensure an economically healthy and globally competitive U.S. air carrier industry and prosperous workforce, including: • Strengthening the competitive position of air carriers to at least ensure equality with foreign air carriers, including the attainment of the opportunity for air carriers to maintain and increase their profitability in foreign air transportation. • Placing maximum reliance on competitive market forces and on actual and potential competition…to provide the needed air transportation system [and] encourage efficient and well-managed air carriers to earn adequate profits and attract capital. • Promoting, encouraging and developing civil aeronautics and a viable, privately owned United States air transport industry. • Encouraging fair wages and working conditions.[b]	According to DOT officials, DOT reviewed its process for conducting a public interest analysis of alliance applications and has conducted outreach to get the perspectives of airlines and labor stakeholders during DOT's review of specific industry actions. For example, DOT officials stated they conducted outreach to pilot unions, and subsequently and separately, pilot unions participated in proceedings concerning antitrust immunity (e.g., the pilot union for Delta Air Lines filed comments in support of Delta's alliance with Virgin Australia.) DOT officials stated that this outreach helped the department better communicate its approach to these reviews. DOT officials stated that they continue to focus on the statutory goals when conducting the public interest analysis. They also noted that their review of alliances is not formulaic and that when issuing an order on a specific alliance, DOT explains the public interest analysis it conducted during the review.
Build upon and expand the DOT's Open Skies initiative, focusing on: (1) the largest and fastest-growing international markets that remain constrained by restrictive bilateral aviation agreements; (2) ensuring de facto market access and a level playing field for U.S. passenger and cargo air carriers facing impediments to doing business abroad; and (3) promoting employment opportunities for U.S. air carrier workers.	Since the issuance of the FAAC report, DOT reached new Open Skies agreements with additional countries, including those with Sierra Leone and Macedonia. These agreements bring the total number of Open Skies partners to 110, as of May 6, 2013. DOT officials told us they are continuing their efforts to establish Open Skies agreements or significant liberalization agreements with China, Mexico, Argentina, South Africa, and Russia. They also said that DOT may use its regulatory authority to redress unfair or discriminatory practices by foreign governments or entities against U.S. interests. For example, on March 15, 2013, DOT issued a "show cause" order related to Italian airport fees.[c] DOT officials noted that they continually work with foreign governments to address unfair or discriminatory practices, but issues rarely rise to the level of requiring formal regulatory action by DOT.

FAAC recommendation—global competitiveness	DOT/FAA actions
Leverage the Secretary of Transportation's appointment to the President's Export Promotion Cabinet, and support an expansion of the DOT's role in promoting aviation exports for U.S. air carriers, manufacturers, and airports, and facilitating international tourism.	The Secretary serves on the President's Export Promotion Cabinet, and DOT is also part of a working group for the National Export Initiative. This initiative was established in 2010 to support trade promotion, is led by the Secretary of Commerce, and includes representatives from the United States Trade Representative, Department of State, and the U.S. Trade and Development Agency. The initiative includes an emphasis on addressing aerospace market access and infrastructure issues, seeking to establish Open Skies agreements and eliminate restrictive aviation practices worldwide. Removal of such restrictions could allow U.S. airlines to more fully participate in the transport of U.S. exports overseas.

Source: FAAC report and GAO analysis of DOT documents and interviews.

[a]See, Statement of United States International Air Transportation Policy, 60 Fed. Reg. 21,841 (May 3, 1995). The FAAC subcommittee was unable to reach consensus supporting the 1995 Policy Statement's objective of reducing existing limitations on cross-border investments.

[b]49 U.S.C. § 40101(a).

[c]Specifically, DOT reached the tentative conclusion that Italian airport authorities charge air carriers operating flights to and from points outside the European Union a different, higher, set of fees than carriers operating flights within the European Union. DOT stated that this imposed an unjustifiable or unreasonable restriction on access of U.S. air carriers to the Italy market and violated the U.S.-EU Air Transport Agreement. If DOT finalizes the order, it will impose operational restrictions on the Italian carrier, Alitalia, forbidding it to engage in air service between Italy and the United States.

DOT's and FAA's Planned Actions

DOT officials noted that they are working to ingrain these recommendations into their existing efforts and processes. They stated that DOT continues to pursue Open Skies agreements with China, Mexico, Argentina, South Africa, and Russia, but given the nature of negotiating such agreements, there is no timetable for concluding these discussions. DOT is also considering a "best practices" template outlining how to implement Open Skies provisions in other countries but has not set a timeframe for finalizing this template.

FAAC Members' Assessment of DOT's and FAA's Progress

Of the nine FAAC competitiveness subcommittee members, two members felt that the recommendation was addressed; six members felt that the recommendation was not fully addressed, and one did not express an opinion. The members who did not feel the recommendation was addressed cited the ongoing nature of competitiveness issues and, in some cases, simply suggested DOT continue its current efforts. However, in other cases, members suggested DOT take additional actions to address the recommendation, for example:

- Three subcommittee members stated additional action should be taken with respect to DOT's work with the Departments of State,

Homeland Security, and Commerce on the National Export Cabinet. Two members stated that the agencies should work to make it easier for tourists and business travelers to obtain visas, and another member noted the need to ensure U.S. carriers receive the same opportunities overseas that foreign carriers receive in the U.S. market.

- Three members stated that DOT should take a more aggressive approach when addressing anti-competitive practices by other countries and supporting the U.S. aviation industry. One subcommittee member stated that DOT needs to refocus on its statutory mandate to strengthen the competitive position of air carriers to at least ensure equality with foreign air carriers; and that the federal government should pursue a national airline policy to follow through on this and other FAAC recommendations. Another member noted that concerns remain with respect to equal access to airport slots during popular travel times while the third member said that DOT should push harder to get an agreement in place with China.

In addition, two subcommittee members, including one that felt the recommendation was addressed, emphasized the need for DOT to consider the labor impacts of Open Skies agreements and the resulting alliances between U.S. and foreign carriers.[41] Another member noted the need to consider the safety impacts. These members noted a lack of consensus during the FAAC discussions regarding how DOT should address these issues; as a result, these issues are not included in the FAAC recommendation but were discussed in the FAAC report as "other areas of significant discussion."[42]

---

[41]These FAAC members noted that during the development of the FAAC report, there were concerns regarding the U.S. labor impacts of an agreement between United Airlines and Aer Lingus to share profits for a route between Washington, D.C. and Madrid. United marketed the flight and Aer Lingus operated it.

[42]The FAAC recommendation stated that DOT should consider existing statutory criteria, which includes encouraging fair wage and working conditions, when conducting its public interest analysis. However, the discussion of the specific issues raised by the FAAC members we interviewed were included in the "Other Areas of Significant Discussion" section of the report, under "Outsourcing" and "Incorporating Core Workers' Human Rights Conventions into International Aviation Trade Agreements." DOT, *The Future of Aviation Advisory Committee Final Report* (Washington, D.C.: Apr. 11, 2011).

Challenges in Implementing the Recommendation	• **Obtaining consensus from many stakeholders, including foreign governments**. DOT officials and four FAAC subcommittee members noted challenges in negotiating Open Skies agreements with other countries—a process that can take many years and ultimately depends on securing the agreement of another nation. Two subcommittee members also noted that addressing competitiveness issues involves input from a number of other stakeholders with conflicting viewpoints, including airlines, airports, labor, other government agencies, and elected officials. As previously noted, DOT officials stated that they had established a dialogue with stakeholders regarding impediments to the implementation of alliances around the world, and conducted outreach to get airlines' and labor stakeholders' perspectives on DOT's public interest analysis of alliances.

Related Products

Slot-Controlled Airports: FAA's Rules Could be Improved to Enhance Competition and Use of Available Capacity. GAO-12-902. Washington, D.C.: September 13, 2012.

Airline Industry: Potential Mergers and Acquisitions Driven by Financial and Competitive Pressures. GAO-08-845. Washington, D.C.: July 31, 2008.

U.S. Aerospace Industry: Progress in Implementing Aerospace Commission Recommendations, and Remaining Challenges. GAO-06-920. Washington, D.C.: September 13, 2006.

Transatlantic Aviation: Effects of Easing Restrictions on U.S.-European Markets. GAO-04-835. Washington, D.C.: July 21, 2004.

Issues Relating to Foreign Investment and Control of U.S. Airlines. GAO-04-34R. Washington, D.C.: October 30, 2003.

International Aviation: DOT's Efforts to Promote U.S. Air Cargo Carriers' Interests. GAO/RCED-97-13. Washington, D.C.: October 18, 1996.

7. FAAC Recommendation— STEM Education

Issue Overview

Aviation and aerospace employers, including government transportation agencies, airlines, and manufacturers, are facing a number of workforce challenges, such as an aging workforce, a lack of needed skills in the current and future workforce, and the need to adapt to rapidly evolving technology and compete in a global marketplace. A number of organizations, including the FAAC, have noted that addressing these challenges will require a focus on science, technology, engineering, and mathematics (STEM) education. The challenges faced by aviation and aerospace employers reflect a larger national trend, as research has shown that the United States lacks a strong pipeline of future workers in STEM fields and that U.S. students continue to lag behind students in other highly technological nations in mathematics and science achievement.

For over three decades, Congress and the executive branch have continued to create new STEM education programs, even though, as we found in 2005, there has been a general lack of assessment of how well STEM programs were working.[43] In January 2012, we reported that thirteen agencies administered 209 STEM education programs in fiscal year 2010 and spent over $3 billion to prepare students and teachers for careers in STEM fields.[44] We noted that the lack of a government-wide strategic plan hampered the effectiveness of the federal effort, and made a number of recommendations related to the larger federal effort on

---

[43]GAO, *Higher Education: Federal Science, Technology, Engineering, and Mathematics Programs and Related Trends*, GAO-06-114 (Washington, D.C.: Oct. 12, 2005).

[44]The number of programs within agencies ranged from 3 to 46, with the Departments of Health and Human Services and Energy and the National Science Foundation administering more than half of these programs. GAO, *Science, Technology, Engineering, and Mathematics Education: Strategic Planning Needed to Better Manage Overlapping Programs across Multiple Agencies*, GAO-12-108 (Washington, D.C.: Jan. 20, 2012)

STEM, which is described in more detail in the next paragraph.[45] Last year, the Office of Management and Budget established a cross-agency priority goal to improve the quality of STEM education at all levels.[46] In May 2012, we reported that by naming STEM education as a cross-agency goal, the administration is taking the first step towards creating a government-wide plan to achieve its goal. However, we also stated that a number of limitations could hamper progress, such as overlapping STEM programs; agencies that did not connect STEM education activities to agency goals in their annual performance plans or measure the progress of their STEM activities; and a lack of information about the effectiveness of STEM programs. We reiterated our prior recommendations.[47]

In addition, the America COMPETES Reauthorization Act of 2010 called for the Office of Science and Technology Policy's (OSTP) National Science and Technology Council (NSTC) to establish a committee to inventory, review, and coordinate federal STEM education programs.[48] The Committee on Science, Technology, Engineering, and Math Education (CoSTEM) is comprised of representatives from eleven

---

[45]We previously recommended that as the Office of Science and Technology Policy (OSTP) leads the government-wide STEM education strategic planning effort, it should (1) work with agencies to better align their activities with a government-wide strategy, (2) develop a plan for sustained coordination, (3) identify programs for potential consolidation or elimination, and (4) assist agencies in determining how to better evaluate their programs. OSTP stated that it would address our recommendations in the 5-year federal STEM Education Strategic Plan. As part of our ongoing work on duplication, overlap, and fragmentation, we report on the status of OSTP's efforts on these items through our action tracker (http://www.gao.gov/duplication/action_tracker). As of March 6, 2013, item 3 is addressed, item 1 is partially addressed, and items 2 and 4 are not addressed.

[46]The GPRA Modernization Act of 2010, Pub. L. No. 111–352, § 5, 124 Stat. 3866, 3873 (Jan. 4, 2011), codified at 31 U.S.C. § 1120, requires that OMB, in coordination with agencies and in consultation with Congress, develop long-term goals for a limited number of crosscutting policy areas and management improvement areas—referred to as cross-agency priority goals—every 4 years.

[47]GAO, *Managing for Results: GAO's Work Related to the Interim Crosscutting Priority Goals under the GPRA Modernization Act*, GAO-12-620R (Washington, D.C.: May 31, 2012). GAO also discussed STEM education in GAO, *2012 Annual Report: Opportunities to Reduce Duplication, Overlap and Fragmentation, Achieve Savings, and Enhance Revenue*, GAO-12-342SP (Washington, D.C.: Feb. 28, 2012).

[48]America COMPETES Reauthorization Act of 2010, Pub. L. No. 111-358, 124 Stat. 3982 (2011).

agencies, including DOT.[49] In December 2011, CoSTEM published an inventory of the federal STEM education portfolio. In May 2013, CoSTEM released a 5-year strategic federal STEM education plan. DOT officials told us that DOT's Research and Innovative Technology Administration (RITA) represents DOT on the CoSTEM effort, and participated in the development of an inventory of federal STEM programs and the development of the Federal STEM education plan. The bulk of DOT's and FAA's activities that are related to STEM education are conducted through FAA's Aviation and Space Education (STEM-AVSED) outreach program. STEM-AVSED's goals include encouraging students to explore aviation and aerospace career opportunities; promoting the skills and knowledge critical to aviation safety; and increasing awareness and understanding of the agency's role in aviation and aerospace.[50]

DOT's and FAA's Actions to Address Recommendation

DOT and FAA officials have taken steps to address the wide-ranging actions identified in the recommendation by improving internal coordination, collaborating with external stakeholders, and conducting STEM outreach to educational institutions and students through a variety of programs. Table 10 provides a summary of the FAAC recommendation on STEM outreach and DOT's and FAA's actions to address it, as of June 2013.

[49]CoSTEM members include the Departments of Agriculture, Commerce, Defense, Education, Energy, Health and Human Services, Interior, Transportation, as well as the Environmental Protection Agency, National Aeronautics and Space Administration, and National Science Foundation.

[50]STEM-AVSED was established in response to Pub. L. No. 94-353, § 21, 90 Stat. 871 (1976), which empowered the FAA Administrator to establish a civil aviation information distribution program to provide state and local school administrators, college and university officials, and officers of civil and other interested organizations with informational materials and expertise on civil aviation..

Table 10: FAAC Recommendation on STEM Outreach and DOT's and FAA's Actions to Address It, as of June 2013

FAAC recommendation—STEM	DOT/FAA actions
Ensure coordination and focus within DOT on workforce development of STEM as a centralized and focused top-tier initiative of the DOT.	According to FAA officials, FAA established a STEM Council that meets monthly to coordinate STEM activities across FAA's business lines. DOT officials stated that it has an internal group that meets 8 to 12 times per year to discuss workforce development, including retraining and succession planning, and that STEM issues are frequently discussed during these meetings.
Assign the Assistant Secretary for Administration the task of developing, overseeing, coordinating, implementing, and integrating a strategic workforce development plan that includes STEM education programs and activities for the current and future workforce.	DOT has not developed a strategic workforce development plan that includes STEM education. DOT officials stated that DOT's next strategic plan, scheduled to be released in 2015, may include some STEM components.
Create an advisory council comprised of outside experts, focused on aviation and aerospace, who can provide expertise to help identify, align, and coordinate efforts on workforce development and STEM education within the DOT.	DOT has not created an advisory council of external aviation and aerospace experts because, according to DOT officials, STEM education is not part of DOT's mission, making it difficult to establish a STEM council under the Federal Advisory Committee Act. DOT officials noted that DOT and FAA partner with outside stakeholders on workforce development and STEM issues through a number of programs, such as the University Transportation Centers Program.[a]
Increase education outreach from pre-kindergarten to institutions of higher education.	FAA officials noted that they continued their outreach to educational institutions through the Aviation and Space Education (STEM-AVSED) program. FAA updated its STEM-AVSED website, which is designed to appeal to an audience unfamiliar with aviation, such as students and teachers. FAA officials stated they plan to augment the existing STEM-AVSED efforts to target middle and high school students with additional programs for elementary students. FAA also developed and distributed a brochure on aviation engineering careers. FAA worked with the National Aeronautics and Space Administration to develop an educational program called Smart Skies that uses an air traffic control simulator to teach algebra. According to FAA, this program has been rolled out to hundreds of schools. FAA worked with DOT to develop the Real World Design Challenge, which is a free engineering competition, and FAA and the Federal Highway Administration are collaborating to combine two youth summer programs: the Aviation Career Education (ACE) Academy[b] and the National Transportation Summer Institute.[c] FAA and its partners developed Ask Polaris, a website designed to help graduating high school students learn more about the field of aerospace engineering, including the types of college degrees available. DOT also established a Youth Employee STEM Mentoring Program, through which DOT mentors work 2 hours per week assisting students with these subjects.

FAAC recommendation—STEM	DOT/FAA actions
Consider improving programs and connections with 2- and 4-year educational institutions that give students hands-on experience applicable to the aviation and aerospace workplace.	FAA officials stated they improved lines of communication with the Centers of Excellence, which award aerospace research grants to colleges. Also, FAA has an MOU to increase the visibility of technical careers in aviation and aerospace with the National Coalition of Certification Centers (NC3), a network of schools and industry leaders that develop aviation certifications. As part of this effort, FAA and NC3 developed a brochure on aviation careers for college recruiters to share with high school counselors, embarked on a national poster campaign—Yes I Can Do That, and implemented a job shadowing program called Walk in Your Boots.
Establish an award for innovation to recognize persons, businesses, or organizations that develop unique scientific and engineering innovations in aerospace and aviation.	DOT established the Secretary's Recognizing Aviation and Aerospace Innovation in Science and Engineering (RAISE) award to recognize innovative scientific and engineering achievements that will have a significant impact on the future of aerospace or aviation. The award is open to students at the high school, undergraduate, and graduate levels. DOT awarded its first RAISE award in October 2012.
Work with the Secretary of Labor as an integral part of the Interagency Aerospace Revitalization Task Force, originally established in 2006, to implement a national strategy focused on recruiting, training, and cultivating the aerospace workforce. Work with the Department of Education to provide resources that would create state-of-the-art STEM elementary and secondary educational facilities.	DOT officials noted that while the Interagency Aerospace Revitalization Task Force was disbanded, DOT has held semiannual Aviation Industry Workforce-Management Conferences with the Departments of Labor and Education. In addition, in September 2011, the Secretaries of Transportation, Education, and Labor signed a memorandum of understanding to collaborate on implementing strategies for using STEM education to develop a qualified aerospace workforce. DOT officials stated that the agencies developed an informal work plan, and have coordinated on efforts to provide information on transportation careers for the Department of Labor's American Job Centers. In addition, as previously mentioned, RITA represents DOT on a federal agency-wide effort to coordinate STEM programs through the Committee on Science, Technology, Engineering, and Math Education.

Source: FAAC report and GAO analysis of DOT and FAA documents and interviews.

[a]RITA's University Transportation Centers program provides grants for universities to operate centers that: advance U.S. technology and expertise in transportation through research, education, workforce development, and technology transfer; provide a critical transportation knowledge base outside the US DOT; and address vital workforce needs for the next generation of transportation leaders.

[b]ACE Academies are interactive aviation summer camps geared towards middle and high school students who are interested in aviation and aerospace.

[c]The National Transportation Summer Institute program is designed to introduce secondary school students to all modes of transportation careers and encourage them to pursue transportation-related courses of study at the college and university level.

DOT's and FAA's Planned Actions

DOT officials stated that the spirit and intent of the recommendation have been addressed, but added that work will continue as education is an evolving process with new audiences to reach. DOT and FAA officials stated they will continue efforts to coordinate programs, partner with stakeholders, and leverage resources. FAA officials noted that it is important that the agency continue to keep a spotlight on STEM education. To maintain that focus, officials stated that the agency could include FAA's STEM work into FAA's Business Plan Goals. FAA officials stated they would like to eventually augment the existing STEM-AVSED efforts to target middle and high school students with additional programs for elementary students but have not established time frames to do so. DOT officials noted that they are working to determine how to attract students through STEM programs, as well as attracting students more interested in technical training.

FAAC Members' Assessment of DOT's and FAA's Progress

Five of the seven FAAC labor and workforce subcommittee members stated that DOT and FAA had addressed the recommendation, but all of the members stated that the DOT's and FAA's work on this issue should continue. Four of the subcommittee members praised DOT efforts such as establishing the RAISE award or the Aviation Industry Workforce-Management Conferences. Two of the subcommittee members—one that thought the recommendation was addressed and one that did not—stated that DOT and FAA should conduct outreach outside of Washington, D.C., on workforce and STEM issues and made diverse suggestions, including involving FAA regional offices, hosting regional workforce summits, providing a regional RAISE award, and interacting with students in university and high school settings. One of the FAAC members who did not think the recommendation was addressed stated that DOT should provide more detail on what they are doing, and how they are measuring their performance.

Challenges in Implementing the Recommendation

- **Coordinating with larger federal efforts to avoid duplication and leverage resources**. We have previously reviewed STEM programs across the federal government and raised concerns about the patchwork of fragmented and overlapping federal STEM programs, noting that poor coordination among the many agencies that oversee these programs and the lack of a government-wide strategic plan have hampered the effectiveness of the federal effort.[51] Six of the

---

[51]GAO-12-620R, GAO, *Science, Technology, Engineering, and Mathematics Education: Strategic Planning Needed to Better Manage Overlapping Programs across Multiple Agencies*, GAO-12-108 (Washington, D.C.: Jan. 20, 2012), and GAO, *2012 Annual Report: Opportunities to Reduce Duplication, Overlap and Fragmentation, Achieve Savings, and Enhance Revenue*, GAO-12-342SP (Washington, D.C.: Feb. 28, 2012).

seven FAAC subcommittee members we interviewed recognized that STEM education is a broad policy issue, and efforts on this recommendation require collaborating with and maintaining the participation of outside groups, such as other agencies, industry, and other stakeholders. The administration is also taking steps to address these issues through establishing a cross-agency priority goal and creating a 5-year strategic plan for STEM education. As previously noted, RITA has participated in the government-wide effort to coordinate STEM programs.

- **Sustaining long-term efforts**. DOT and FAA officials and a FAAC subcommittee member noted that education is an evolving, ongoing effort, which can be difficult to sustain interest and support for over the long term. They added that funding and limited resources pose challenges to maintaining these efforts, but the agencies work to leverage resources through the partnerships previously noted.

- **Attracting students to aviation careers**. FAA officials stated that attracting students to technical careers can be challenging given misconceptions about aviation maintenance careers. Five of the FAAC subcommittee members also noted the challenges in enticing students into the STEM fields or related aviation careers, and three of the members stated that a viable and sustainable aviation industry would help address this challenge. FAA officials also noted challenges in developing web content that appealed to students and educators while staying within FAA's branding guidelines, which are typically geared toward FAA's traditional audience of aviation professionals. However, FAA officials stated they were working across departments within FAA to address these issues.

Related Products

Science, Technology, Engineering, and Mathematics Education: Governmentwide Strategy Needed to Better Manage Overlapping Programs. GAO-13-529T. Washington, D.C.: April 10, 2013.

Aviation Safety: Additional FAA Efforts Could Enhance Safety Risk Management. GAO-12-898. Washington, D.C.: September 12, 2012.

Managing for Results: GAO's Work Related to the Interim Crosscutting Priority Goals under the GPRA Modernization Act. GAO-12-620R. Washington, D.C.: May 31, 2012.

2012 Annual Report Opportunities to Reduce Duplication, Overlap and Fragmentation, Achieve Savings, and Enhance Revenue. GAO-12-342SP. Washington, D.C.: February 28, 2012.

Science, Technology, Engineering, and Mathematics Education: Strategic Planning Needed to Better Manage Overlapping Programs across Multiple Agencies. GAO-12-108. Washington, D.C.: January 20, 2012.

Federal Aviation Administration: Agency Is Taking Steps to Plan for and Train Its Technician Workforce, but a More Strategic Approach Is Warranted. GAO-11-91. Washington, D.C.: October 22, 2010.

8. FAAC Recommendation— Legal Protections for Safety Data

Issue Overview

For decades, FAA and the aviation industry have used data to identify the causes of aviation accidents and incidents and take actions to prevent their recurrence. Our prior work has shown that FAA is in the midst of a shift toward a proactive, data-driven safety oversight approach, commonly referred to as a safety management system (SMS) approach.[52] Under this new approach, FAA plans to use aviation safety data to identify system-wide trends in aviation safety and manage emerging hazards before they result in incidents or accidents.

In addition to mandatory reporting systems and inspection programs that collect information on safety issues and events, FAA has developed a number of voluntary reporting systems that air carrier and industry personnel can use to report safety issues and events.[53] For example, FAA's Aviation Safety Action Program (ASAP) allows air carrier employees to voluntarily report safety issues and events and provides protection from enforcement action by FAA and disciplinary action by airline management or others. To improve FAA's capability for automated

---

[52]We have previously reported on FAA's implementation of SMS. See GAO, *Aviation Safety: FAA Efforts Have Improved Safety but Challenges Remain in Key Areas*, GAO-13-442T (Washington, D.C.: Apr 16, 2013); GAO, *Aviation Safety: Additional FAA Efforts Could Enhance Safety Risk Management*, GAO-12-898 (Washington, D.C.: Sept 12, 2012); GAO, *Aviation Safety: FAA Is Taking Steps to Improve Data, but Challenges for Managing Safety Risks Remain*, GAO-12-660T, (Washington, D.C.: Apr 25, 2012); and GAO, *Aviation Safety: Improved Data Quality and Analysis Capabilities Are Needed as FAA Plans a Risk-Based Approach to Safety Oversight*, GAO-10-414 (Washington, D.C.: May 6, 2010).

[53]One example of a mandatory system is the Air Traffic Quality Assurance database, which contains information recorded by air traffic controller supervisors, support specialists, and managers. With respect to inspections, FAA records data from maintenance and operations inspections in the Air Transportation Oversight System (ATOS). Under the ATOS concept, FAA inspectors use data analysis to focus their inspections on areas that pose the greatest risk. ATOS also permits inspectors to shift the focus of their inspections in response to changing conditions within air carriers' operations.

analysis of multiple databases, FAA has partnered with industry through the Aviation Safety Information Analysis and Sharing (ASIAS) program. According to FAA documents, ASIAS leverages data from multiple sources, including FAA data sets, airline proprietary safety data, publicly available data, and manufacturer data, allowing FAA to (1) perform integrated queries across multiple databases, (2) search an extensive warehouse of safety data, and (3) display pertinent elements in an array of useful formats. The ASIAS home page shows that as of February 2013, 44 airlines were participating in ASIAS, including 13 of the 14 airlines with at least 1 percent of total domestic scheduled passenger service revenue. FAA is also in two rulemaking processes to require SMS—which will include the development of systems for reporting, tracking, and analyzing safety data—for air carriers and airports.

Our prior work has shown that the success of a SMS program depends upon the open sharing of safety information among aviation stakeholders; however, FAA officials have recognized that aviation industry concerns about data protection and legal liability could hinder the implementation of SMS.[54] The FAAC stated that the development, analysis, and availability of shared safety information could be inhibited by the potential that this information may be used for other purposes, such as exposure through the media, admissions in criminal or administrative prosecution, or use in civil litigation.

DOT's and FAA's Actions to Address Recommendation

Table 11 provides a summary of the FAAC recommendation to ensure safety data protections and DOT's and FAA's actions to address it, as of June 2013.

---

[54]GAO-12-898.

Table 11: FAAC Recommendation on Safety Data Protections and DOT's and FAA's Actions to Address It, as of June 2013

FAAC recommendation—data protection	DOT/FAA actions
Seek comprehensive legal protection for participants in voluntary and mandated safety management system (SMS) data programs to ensure the programs' continued benefits to safety, pursue essential legislative action that is vital to provide ongoing protection of safety information-sharing systems in the United States, and work with Congress to introduce such legislation at the earliest possible opportunity.	Since the FAAC report was issued, Congress passed the FAA Modernization and Reform Act.[a] This Act prohibits the public disclosure by FAA of data and information submitted voluntarily to FAA and developed under the following programs: Aviation Safety Action Program; Flight Operational Quality Assurance Program; and Line Operations Safety Audit Program, as well as reports, data or other information produced or collected for purposes of developing and implementing a SMS program, and reports based thereon, including reports under the Aviation Safety Information Analysis and Sharing (ASIAS) Program.
	FAA officials stated they provided technical assistance to Congress on this issue. FAA officials also noted that FAA is involved in an ICAO task force that is developing standards and recommended practices related to safety data including guidance for judiciary bodies on the issue of protecting safety data during litigation.

Source: FAAC report and GAO analysis of DOT and FAA documents and interviews.

[a]Pub. L. No. 112-95, § 310, 126 Stat. 11.

DOT's and FAA's Planned Actions

FAA officials consider this recommendation addressed. More specifically, while the FAA Modernization and Reform Act did not prohibit the disclosure of data in civil or criminal litigation, or provide protections if data are submitted through mandatory programs, FAA officials consider the law to address the intent of this recommendation. As previously noted, FAA is in the midst of a rulemaking process to require SMS for air carriers, and FAA officials acknowledged that there are remaining concerns among industry stakeholders regarding the extent to which data collected under mandatory SMS programs would be protected.[55] FAA officials stated they plan to address this issue in the publication of a final rule on SMS implementation by air carriers, which is expected to be

---

[55]The Airline Safety and Federal Aviation Administration Extension Act of 2010, Pub. L. No. 111-216, § 215, 124 Stat. 2348, 2366 (2010), required the FAA to require all part 121 air carriers to implement SMS. In its Notice of Proposed Rulemaking on implementing this requirement, FAA stated that SMS should include systems for safety performance monitoring and measuring, including a confidential employee safety reporting system. FAA noted that while certain voluntary programs, such as the Aviation Safety Action Program (ASAP), would be useful as part of a carrier's SMS system, it would not mandate the use of such programs, as that would result in the data becoming mandatory and thus losing existing statutory protections. 75 Fed. Reg. 68224, 68228 (Nov. 5, 2010). FAA has not issued a final rule.

completed in October 2013. FAA officials also stated they will continue to encourage the voluntary reporting of data into ASIAS.

FAAC Members' Assessment of DOT's and FAA's Progress

The evolving nature of aviation safety and remaining concerns regarding the potential disclosure of data led to varying opinions on the extent to which the recommendation was addressed. Two subcommittee members said it was addressed, with one citing the provisions protecting safety data from disclosure in the FAA Modernization and Reform Act, and another noting the work is ongoing. Four of the seven FAAC safety subcommittee members did not believe that the recommendation was addressed, but three of them noted that work was ongoing or that safety was an evolving issue. One subcommittee member stated he did not have enough information to comment on the status of this recommendation. Three subcommittee members expressed concern on the potential disclosure of data during criminal and civil litigation while another member expressed concern on protecting data that is mandated to be submitted—neither of which is addressed by current law but were included in the FAAC recommendation. One member noted that FAA needs to better communicate to Congress how the lack of protections could have serious ramifications on voluntary reporting of safety data. Two subcommittee members suggested additional areas of focus beyond the recommendation, including collecting data on the amount of time pilots spend flying to the city where they begin their work day—an issue discussed in the aftermath of the 2009 Colgan accident—and the need for international harmonization on the definition of legal protections for safety data.

Challenges in Implementing the Recommendation

- **Addressing remaining data protection concerns**. FAA officials as well as two FAAC subcommittee members acknowledged industry concern with respect to protecting safety data during criminal and civil litigation and recognized its potential impact on SMS implementation. However, they noted that it will be difficult to determine the extent to which this issue could affect SMS and data sharing until it is tested in court. Four of the subcommittee members stated that the potential for disclosure could also affect operators' or their employees' willingness to voluntarily report safety issues.

While protection of airport safety data was not specifically discussed as part of the FAAC's recommendation, we reported in September 2012 that these data are subject to state-specific FOIA laws, which could make air carriers less willing to share safety information with airports.[56] Specifically, while air carriers are not directly subject to state FOIA laws because they are privately owned, data that airports collect and submit to FAA for SMS—such as information on hazards or other safety data—may be subject to public disclosure under state FOIA laws. FAA officials and experts stated that state FOIA laws could affect the willingness of air carriers to share safety data with airports because any data they choose to share with airports could then be subject to these laws. We recommended that the FAA Administrator consider strategies to address airports' concerns, including asking Congress to provide additional protection for SMS data collected by public entities. Officials stated that FAA is working to address this recommendation.

Related Products

Aviation Safety: FAA Efforts Have Improved Safety but Challenges Remain in Key Areas. GAO-13-442T. Washington, D.C.: April 16, 2013.

Aviation Safety: Additional FAA Efforts Could Enhance Safety Risk Management. GAO-12-898. Washington, D.C.: September 12, 2012.

Aviation Safety: FAA Is Taking Steps to Improve Data, but Challenges for Managing Safety Risks Remain. GAO-12-660T. Washington, D.C.: April 25, 2012.

Aviation Safety: Improved Data Quality and Analysis Capabilities Are Needed as FAA Plans a Risk-Based Approach to Safety Oversight. GAO-10-414. Washington, D.C.: May 6, 2010.

---

[56]GAO-12-898. FAA issues airport operating certificates to airports that (1) serve unscheduled air carrier aircraft with more than 30 seats; or (2) serve scheduled air carrier operations in aircraft with more than 9 seats. 14 C.F.R. § 139.1(a). Most certificated U.S. airports are either owned by a state, a subdivision of a state, or a local government body, and thus are subject to state laws, including state FOIA laws.

9. FAAC Recommendation— Predictive Analytic Capabilities for Safety Data and Information

Issue Overview

As previously noted, FAA is in the midst of a shift toward a proactive, data-driven safety oversight approach, commonly referred to as a safety management system (SMS) approach. Under this new approach, FAA plans to use aviation safety data to identify system-wide trends in aviation safety and manage emerging hazards before they result in incidents or accidents. The FAAC noted that to develop the robust predictive risk-discovery capabilities needed for SMS, FAA must develop advanced analytical tools and methods, as well as modeling and simulation capabilities. According to FAA, the Aviation Safety Information Analysis and Sharing (ASIAS) program—a joint industry and FAA effort that serves as a central exchange of safety information—is a cornerstone of its effort to implement SMS. According to FAA documents, ASIAS leverages data from multiple sources—including FAA data sets, airline proprietary safety data, publicly available data, and manufacturer data—allowing FAA to (1) perform integrated queries across multiple databases, (2) search an extensive warehouse of safety data, and (3) display pertinent elements in an array of useful formats. The ASIAS home page shows that as of February 2013, 44 airlines were participating in ASIAS.

According to the FAAC, the initial results of ASIAS analyses have demonstrated the value of using safety information to produce a system safety baseline. However, the FAAC noted that realization of predictive safety risk-discovery requires investment in expanding, accelerating, and maturing ASIAS capabilities.

DOT's and FAA's Actions to Address Recommendation

Table 12 provides a summary of the FAAC recommendation on developing predictive safety risk analysis capabilities and FAA's actions to address it, as of June 2013.

Table 12: FAAC Recommendation on Predictive Analytic Capabilities for Safety Data and Information and DOT's and FAA's Actions to Address It, as of June 2013

FAAC recommendation—predictive capabilities	DOT/FAA actions
Provide focus, priority, and resources to develop improved tools and methods that will result in robust predictive analytic capabilities for safety data and information.	Consistent with the FAAC's recommendation, FAA has pursued action to expand and support Aviation Safety Information Analysis and Sharing (ASIAS). In 2011, the ASIAS program received FAA approval for $15 million per year[a] for 5 years (fiscal years 2013 through 2017) to collect additional data and further develop its analytical capabilities in support of a more proactive safety management approach. For example, according to FAA, there are efforts under way to add air-traffic-control voice data and general aviation data to ASIAS, which currently includes airline-collected data, data from the voluntary Flight Operational Quality Assurance (FOQA) program, pilot-provided data, weather data, air traffic control-generated data, and radar-tracking data. FAA is also working with three airlines to demonstrate the modeling capabilities of ASIAS if more airline-provided data were combined with FAA data sources. According to its current plan, by 2017, FAA would like to deploy modeling capabilities that cover all phases of flight and to have developed and refined risk models that incorporate the risk factors developed through the identification and validation of safety issues, accident precursors, and other vulnerabilities.

Source: FAAC report and GAO analysis of DOT and FAA documents and interviews.

[a]Though ASIAS received approval for these funds, funds must still be appropriated for ASIAS on an annual basis.

DOT's and FAA's Planned Actions

By securing the funds for execution, FAA believes that it has fulfilled the spirit of the recommendation and is positioned to deliver predictive safety risk-discovery capabilities. Officials told us that FAA intends to continue executing its 5-year ASIAS Plan.

FAAC Members' Assessment of DOT's and FAA's Progress

While six of the FAAC safety subcommittee members who provided an opinion stated that FAA's efforts to address this recommendation would be ongoing, members varied in their opinion as to whether the recommendation was fully addressed. One subcommittee member stated he did not have enough information to comment on the status of this recommendation. Two subcommittee members stated it was fully addressed because FAA has secured the resources currently needed for ASIAS, but noted that the nature of the recommendation meant the work and support would need to be ongoing. Four members did not feel the recommendation was fully addressed, and three noted this was due to the ongoing nature of the recommendation, but stated that they were satisfied with FAA's actions.[57] For example, one subcommittee member said that developing predictive safety risk-discovery capabilities requires constantly refining and making the capabilities more sophisticated.

Challenges in Implementing the Recommendation

- **Data protection.** FAA officials and FAAC members noted that addressing the FAAC's other safety data-related recommendations—that is, to expand its collection of voluntary safety data sources and to legally protect that information—will affect the development of predictive capabilities.[58] Two subcommittee members stated FAA should highlight the benefits of data-sharing systems, such as improved safety outcomes, to encourage more participation in such programs. Three FAAC subcommittee members noted the need to address legal concerns regarding data protection.

- **Data quality.** According to FAA, simply collecting the data is not enough; once collected, the data need to be of reliable quality and share a common lexicon and format across contributors.[59] For example, FAA's ASIAS plan explains that since ASIAS pulls data from a number of sources, it is important to ensure that a data element from one source represents the same issue as a data element from another source. One FAAC subcommittee member noted that FAA will need to address this issue in order to develop methods to automatically mine the data (i.e., use computer programs to identify patterns and trends in the data), since having a systematic method to analyze the data would further enable FAA's ability to use ASIAS data

---

[57]Another subcommittee member had underlying concerns regarding FAA's oversight of airlines and felt those should be addressed. These concerns were not discussed in the FAAC report's discussion of the recommendation, but were discussed in the "Other Areas of Significant Discussion" section of the report, under "Safety And Security Of Contract Maintenance Facilities." DOT, *The Future of Aviation Advisory Committee Final Report* (Washington, D.C.: Apr. 11, 2011).

[58]The FAAC report included a recommendation for DOT and FAA to work with stakeholders to identify potential new sources of safety data to be included in voluntary data-sharing programs. While we did not review DOT's and FAA's progress on this recommendation, we did review their progress in addressing the FAAC recommendation on protecting safety data from disclosure: see the discussion of recommendation 8.

[59]GAO has previously commented on and made recommendations about the data quality issues. See GAO-13-442T, GAO-13-36, GAO-12-898, GAO-12-660T, and GAO-10-414.

to proactively identify risks. According to its ASIAS Plan, FAA will address and monitor these issues regularly as new data sources are added. It plans to develop taxonomies to better merge data from programs like ASAP, the Air Traffic Safety Action Program, and FOQA in 2013 and 2014.

- **Resource constraints**. Three FAAC subcommittee members raised concerns about how budget issues would affect FAA's efforts to implement the recommendation. One subcommittee member noted that making substantive progress on this recommendation will not be possible until budget issues are addressed. According to FAA officials, funding reductions due to sequestration will not have a major effect on the program's development in fiscal year 2013. However, the officials noted that these reductions will delay some specific improvements, such as ASIAS's ability to detect instances where aircraft situational awareness is lost.

- **Analytical capabilities**. According to FAA officials, labor agreements and other factors can affect the agency's ability to fully develop the analytical capabilities of ASIAS. For example, the ASIAS Executive Board must authorize analyses of ASIAS data, and in some cases, the members of the board are constrained by labor agreements that limit how their airlines' data can be used.[60] FAA officials noted that while they provide the airlines with industry benchmarks from ASIAS so the airline can see how it compares on certain metrics, it is unclear how the airlines are using the data. In addition, FAA officials told us that because some of the identifying information is stripped from the data, FAA is limited in its analyses that would indicate the relative safety performance of a particular airline. For example, if the information is left with identifiers, then FAA would be able to pull other relevant reports associated with a particular flight, and could merge that data to understand all the relevant factors, and then de-identify the information. As mentioned in Table 12, FAA stated it is working with three airlines to demonstrate the benefits of using this approach.

Related Products

General Aviation Safety: Additional FAA Efforts Could Help Identify and Mitigate Safety Risks. GAO-13-36. Washington, D.C.: October 4, 2012.

---

[60]ASIAS is governed by an Executive Board comprised of representatives from government and industry.

Aviation Safety: Additional FAA Efforts Could Enhance Safety Risk Management. GAO-12-898. Washington, D.C.: September 12, 2012.

Aviation Safety: FAA Is Taking Steps to Improve Data, but Challenges for Managing Safety Risks Remain. GAO-12-660T. Washington, D.C.: April 25, 2012.

Aviation Safety: Improved Data Quality and Analysis Capabilities Are Needed as FAA Plans a Risk-Based Approach to Safety Oversight. GAO-10-414. Washington, D.C.: May 6, 2010.

10. FAAC Recommendation— Prioritize Rulemaking

Issue Overview

The safety of the nation's flying public depends, in large part, on the aviation industry's compliance with safety regulations and FAA's enforcement of those regulations when violations occur. As part of FAA's oversight of aviation safety, FAA develops rules and regulations through the rulemaking process.[61] FAA, the National Transportation Safety Board (NTSB), and we have previously expressed concerns about the efficiency and timeliness of FAA's rulemaking efforts.[62] In 2010, we noted that a number of issues may contribute to a lengthy rulemaking process at FAA, including the need to conduct research, obtain public comment, and provide industry time to comply with the rule. In addition, we reported that external pressures—such as highly publicized accidents, recommendations by NTSB, and congressional mandates—as well as internal pressures, such as changes in management's emphasis, continued to add to and shift the agency's priorities, and that shifting priorities can add to delays. The FAAC report raised similar concerns, stating that the queue of potential rulemaking projects far exceeds the FAA capacity for action in a reasonable time period, and there does not appear to be a universally understood methodology for FAA to ensure the most effective projects receive the highest priority.

Historically, FAA attempted to gain the industry's compliance with rules and regulations through enforcement tools, including levying fines and

---

[61]The basic process by which agencies develop and issue regulations is spelled out in the Administrative Procedure Act (5 U.S.C. §§ 551–570a.) Although there are exceptions, rulemaking generally involves the agency publishing a notice of proposed rulemaking and asking for public comment, then issuing a final rule and responding to the public comments received. A need for rulemaking can be identified internally, by one of FAA's offices, or externally, by an outside source such as the Congress or the National Transportation Safety Board, which issues mandates or recommendations, respectively, calling for rulemaking.

[62]GAO, *Aviation Rulemaking: Further Reform Is Needed to Address Long-standing Problems*, GAO-01-821 (Washington, D.C.: July 9, 2001) and *Aviation Safety: Improved Planning Could Help FAA Address Challenges Related to Winter Weather Operations*, GAO-10-678 (Washington, D.C.: July 29, 2010).

suspending or revoking operating certificates. However, as previously noted, FAA and the U.S. aviation industry are moving toward the adoption of safety management systems (SMS)—a data-driven, risk-based safety oversight approach. The FAAC report raised concerns that FAA's enforcement policies are not reflective of the shift to SMS, because FAA focuses its enforcement on regulatory non-compliance, regardless of risk level, rather than prioritizing its efforts to address unacceptable risks.

DOT's and FAA's Actions to Address Recommendation

Table 13 provides a summary of the FAAC recommendation to review FAA's rulemaking priorities and FAA's actions to address it, as of June 2013.

Table 13: FAAC Recommendation on Rulemaking Priorities and DOT's and FAA's Actions to Address It, as of June 2013

FAAC recommendation—rulemaking	DOT/FAA actions
Promptly review the existing regulatory and safety initiative calendar to provide parameters and criteria for the FAA to prioritize its current and future rulemaking program. This review should include industry, or at a minimum seek industry input, and the results be made publicly available. In addition, FAA should review field safety and enforcement policies, procedures, and training to ensure they align with the safety management system (SMS) philosophies and supporting policies established by FAA.	To address this recommendation, FAA tasked the Aviation Rulemaking Advisory Committee (ARAC) on March 30, 2011, to provide advice and recommendations on how to prioritize rulemaking projects. The ARAC, in turn, established the Rulemaking Prioritization Working Group (RPWG) to conduct its task. The RPWG developed a rulemaking prioritization model to collect and analyze information to prioritize rulemaking projects. The model includes: • A 3-part questionnaire that ensures that the problem is defined and factual data are gathered so that weighting and scoring of the problem and potential solution can take place; and • A tool that uses the results of the questionnaire to weight and score the problem and potential solution within the following attributes: safety, environment, capacity, access, international, cost/impact, benefit, technology, legislative mandate, social impacts, and security effects. From May to October 2012, the RPWG and FAA subject matter experts tested the model by applying it to 12 final rules. As a result of the testing, the RPWG made improvements to the model. The RPWG submitted a final report recommending that FAA adopt the model across its lines of business. FAA accepted the recommendation report on January 31, 2013, and the Office of Rulemaking formed an implementation team, which drafted a plan outlining the process for implementing the RPWG's recommendation. FAA officials stated that the implementation team developed a tool that will provide a standardized basis for evaluating and prioritizing potential projects. The tool will be used by each line of business to evaluate potential rulemaking projects for the next fiscal year and will serve as the basis in establishing FAA's forecast list of potential rulemaking projects, which will replace the existing 4-Year Look Ahead.[a] With respect to aligning enforcement policies with SMS, FAA officials told us that because SMS was addressed by an earlier Aviation Rulemaking Committee and FAA was in the early stages of determining its SMS policy when the RPWG was tasked, SMS was not addressed by the RPWG. In 2012, FAA issued an order establishing a safety risk management policy for FAA and, according to FAA officials, the rulemaking prioritization team has included safety risk management questions in its tool.

Source: FAAC report and GAO analysis of DOT and FAA documents and interviews.

[a]The 4-Year Look Ahead provided a list of proposed projects that each line of business was considering for submittal to the rulemaking council to initiate rulemaking.

DOT's and FAA's Planned Actions

Officials from FAA's Office of Rulemaking stated that this recommendation has been addressed through ARAC and added that the implementation team is evaluating how to integrate the recommended model into the current rulemaking process without creating unnecessary redundancies. FAA officials stated they requested external feedback on the model through the ARAC, at ARAC's June 20, 2013, meeting. According to FAA officials, ARAC members generally support implementation activities and FAA is considering the feedback ARAC provided on the tool and future ARAC involvement. FAA plans to beta test the model in June 2013 and fully implement it in fiscal year 2014. FAA officials stated that the current tool is supported by MS Excel, but noted that FAA is developing an automated version of all rulemaking tools and is including the prioritization model in the requirements.

FAAC Members' Assessment of DOT's and FAA's Progress

Four of the six FAAC safety subcommittee members felt the recommendation was not fully addressed; two members felt it was addressed, although one stated that FAA should take additional actions as its work on this recommendation continues, and one member did not provide an opinion. One of the subcommittee members who stated the recommendation was not addressed, as well as one member who stated it was, suggested that FAA should be more transparent about its process. Another subcommittee member felt that FAA should communicate more with the NTSB when prioritizing rulemakings.[63] Another subcommittee member stated FAA was making progress, but he was unsure where FAA was in the process since receiving the recommendations from the ARAC. The remaining member had concerns beyond prioritization of rulemaking, such as the clarity of FAA rules and the role of external input versus data when crafting rules.

Challenges in Implementing the Recommendation

- **Resource constraints**. FAA officials noted that budget constraints could affect their efforts to implement and automate the model. For example, automating the model from current Microsoft Word and Excel files will require funding, though FAA officials stated that they can use an internal system for the initial implementation.

- **Addressing competing interests**. Two FAAC subcommittee members noted that one challenge to implementing a rulemaking

---

[63]This subcommittee member was particularly concerned about FAA's policy regarding child restraint systems in aircraft, which was discussed in the FAAC report under recommendation 23.

prioritization process is appropriately addressing aviation safety issues raised by external parties, such as the public, Congress, the DOT Inspector General, and GAO, without shifting FAA's focus from continuing to address other top priority issues.

- **Culture change**. Two other FAAC subcommittee members noted that implementing this recommendation would require a culture change at FAA, which could be difficult. For example, one stressed the need for FAA to be proactive in addressing safety issues, and the other stated that FAA will need to develop a holistic approach toward rulemaking that allows it to address issues quickly.

Related Products

Federal Rulemaking: Agencies Could Take Additional Steps to Respond to Public Comments. GAO-13-21. Washington, D.C.: December 20, 2012.

Aviation Safety: Additional FAA Efforts Could Enhance Safety Risk Management. GAO-12-898. Washington, D.C.: September 12, 2012.

Aviation Safety: Improved Planning Could Help FAA Address Challenges Related to Winter Weather Operations. GAO-10-678. Washington, D.C.: July 29, 2010.

Aviation Safety: Better Management Controls are Needed to Improve FAA's Safety Enforcement and Compliance Efforts. GAO-04-646. Washington, D.C.: July 6, 2004.

Aviation Rulemaking: Incomplete Implementation Impaired FAA's Reform Efforts. GAO-01-950T. Washington, D.C.: July 11, 2001.

Aviation Rulemaking: Further Reform Is Needed to Address Long-standing Problems. GAO-01-821. Washington, D.C.: July 9, 2001.

Appendix I: Listing of the 23 Recommendations Made by the Future of Aviation Advisory Committee, by Area

Environment

1. Exercise strong national leadership to promote and showcase U.S. aviation as a first user of sustainable alternative fuels.
2. Support research and development related to airframe and engine technologies.
3. Secure operational and infrastructure improvements (NextGen, ground taxi delay management programs, and airport energy efficiency and emissions reduction program).
4. Establish a harmonized approach for aviation carbon dioxide emission reductions.

Financing

5. Support extending the alternative minimum tax exemption for airport private activity bonds.
6. Fund accelerated Next Generation Air Transportation System (NextGen) equipage of aircraft.
7. Deliver the benefits of NextGen.
8. Review eligibility criteria for the Airport Improvement Program and Passenger Facility Charge Program.

Competitiveness and viability

9. Promote the global competitiveness of the U.S. aviation industry.
10. Commission an independent study of federal aviation taxes and fees.
11. Ensure transparency in ticket pricing, fees, code-share, contracts of carriage, and travel statistics.
12. Support intermodalism by establishing a task force, examining the Essential Air Service Program, and recommending that legislation prioritize intermodal links.
13. Reform the Essential Air Service program.
14. Continue to be involved in efforts to address jet fuel price volatility.

Labor and world-class workforce

15. Ensure coordination and focus on science, technology, engineering, and math education programs.
16. Urge the National Mediation Board to implement the Dunlop II recommendations.

**Appendix I: Listing of the 23
Recommendations Made by the Future of
Aviation Advisory Committee, by Area**

17. Implement a semi-annual Aviation Industry Workforce-Management Conference.

Aviation Safety

18. Seek legal protections for safety data program participants.

19. Support predictive analytic capabilities for safety data and information.

20. Identify new sources of safety data and establish criteria for inclusion in voluntary data-sharing programs.

21. Include safety performance standards and training into NextGen planning and implementation.

22. Review and reprioritize FAA's rulemaking initiatives.

23. Address issues related to child safety for air travel.

Appendix II: Future of Aviation Advisory Committee Members

The Department of Transportation (DOT) chartered the Future of Aviation Advisory Committee (FAAC) on April 16, 2010, to develop a manageable, actionable list of recommendations for DOT. The FAAC included 19 representatives —1 government official (DOT Assistant Secretary for Aviation and International Affairs) and 18 non-government representatives—from a cross-section of stakeholders, such as air carriers, airports, airline labor unions, manufacturers, and representatives from the finance community, academia, and passenger interests. The FAAC established five subcommittees to develop recommendations in the five areas of interest specified in the FAAC charter: environment, financing, competitiveness and viability, labor and workforce, and safety. A list of the FAAC members, as well as the subcommittees they served on, is provided in table 14.

Table 14: Non-Government FAAC Members

FAAC member	Groups represented	Subcommittees
Juan J. Alonso, Associate Professor in the Department of Aeronautics & Astronautics, Stanford University	Academic - Environment	Environment Safety
Susan Baer, Director, Aviation Department, Port Authority of New York and New Jersey	Airports	Competitiveness Safety
David Barger, President and CEO, JetBlue Airways Corporation	Airlines	Labor Safety
Bryan Bedford, Chairman, President & CEO, Republic Airways Holdings, Inc.	Airlines	Environment Competitiveness
Severin Borenstein, E.T. Grether Professor of Business Administration and Public Policy at the Haas School of Business and Co-Director of the Energy Institute at Haas, and Director of the University of California Energy Institute	Academic - Economics	Finance Competitiveness
Thella Bowens, President & CEO, San Diego County Regional Airport Authority	Airports	Finance Labor
John Conley, International Administrative Vice President, Transport Workers Union of America, AFL-CIO	Labor	Labor Safety
Cynthia Egnotovich, President for Customer Service, UTC Aerospace Systems	Manufacturers	Environment Labor
Patricia Friend, Retired (former International President, Association of Flight Attendants-CWA, AFL-CIO)	Labor	Competitiveness Labor
Robert Lekites, Executive Vice President, Customers, Airbus (former President of United Parcel Service Airlines)	Airlines	Labor Safety
Ana McAhron-Schulz, Director of Economic and Financial Analysis, Air Line Pilots Association	Labor	Competitiveness Labor

FAAC member	Groups represented	Subcommittees
William McGee, Travel and Aviation Consultant for Consumers Union	Consumers	Competitiveness Safety
Daniel McKenzie, Analyst, Buckingham Research Group	Analyst - Finance	Finance Competitiveness
Jack Pelton, Managing Director for Aviation Alliance LLC (former Chairman, President, and CEO, Cessna Aircraft Company)	General Aviation	Finance Competitiveness
Nicole Piasecki, Vice President for Propulsion, Boeing Commercial Airplanes	Manufacturers	Environment Safety
Raul Regalado, Principal, Raul Regalado and Associates (former President & CEO, Metropolitan Nashville Airport Authority)	Airports	Environment Finance
Glenn Tilton, Vice Chairman at JPMorgan Chase (former Chairman, President & CEO of UAL Corporation—United Airlines)	Airlines	Finance Competitiveness
Christopher J. Williams[a] Chairman, CEO and founder of The Williams Capital Group, L.P. and Williams Capital Management, LLC	Finance	Finance Competitiveness

Source: GAO analysis of DOT documents.

[a]Mr. Williams was not available for an interview.

Appendix III: GAO Contact and Staff Acknowledgments

GAO Contact	Gerald L. Dillingham, Ph.D., (202) 512-2834 or dillinghamg@gao.gov
Staff Acknowledgments	In addition to the contact named above the following individuals made important contributions to this report: Heather Krause (Assistant Director); Amy Abramowitz; Melissa Bodeau; Anne Dore; Kevin Egan; Crystal Huggins; Bert Japikse; Aaron Kaminsky; Bill Keller; Tim Minelli; SaraAnn Moessbauer; Susan Offutt; Paul Revesz; Marylynn Sergent; Gretchen Snoey; Pamela Vines; and Jessica Wintfeld.

GAO's Mission	The Government Accountability Office, the audit, evaluation, and investigative arm of Congress, exists to support Congress in meeting its constitutional responsibilities and to help improve the performance and accountability of the federal government for the American people. GAO examines the use of public funds; evaluates federal programs and policies; and provides analyses, recommendations, and other assistance to help Congress make informed oversight, policy, and funding decisions. GAO's commitment to good government is reflected in its core values of accountability, integrity, and reliability.
Obtaining Copies of GAO Reports and Testimony	The fastest and easiest way to obtain copies of GAO documents at no cost is through GAO's website (http://www.gao.gov). Each weekday afternoon, GAO posts on its website newly released reports, testimony, and correspondence. To have GAO e-mail you a list of newly posted products, go to http://www.gao.gov and select "E-mail Updates."
Order by Phone	The price of each GAO publication reflects GAO's actual cost of production and distribution and depends on the number of pages in the publication and whether the publication is printed in color or black and white. Pricing and ordering information is posted on GAO's website, http://www.gao.gov/ordering.htm. Place orders by calling (202) 512-6000, toll free (866) 801-7077, or TDD (202) 512-2537. Orders may be paid for using American Express, Discover Card, MasterCard, Visa, check, or money order. Call for additional information.
Connect with GAO	Connect with GAO on Facebook, Flickr, Twitter, and YouTube. Subscribe to our RSS Feeds or E-mail Updates. Listen to our Podcasts. Visit GAO on the web at www.gao.gov.
To Report Fraud, Waste, and Abuse in Federal Programs	Contact: Website: http://www.gao.gov/fraudnet/fraudnet.htm E-mail: fraudnet@gao.gov Automated answering system: (800) 424-5454 or (202) 512-7470
Congressional Relations	Katherine Siggerud, Managing Director, siggerudk@gao.gov, (202) 512-4400, U.S. Government Accountability Office, 441 G Street NW, Room 7125, Washington, DC 20548
Public Affairs	Chuck Young, Managing Director, youngc1@gao.gov, (202) 512-4800 U.S. Government Accountability Office, 441 G Street NW, Room 7149 Washington, DC 20548